# DECK SEAMANSHIP

*Also by Colin Jarman*
Modern Rope Seamanship (*with Bill Beavis*) (Adlard Coles Ltd)
Coastal Cruising (A. & C. Black)

# DECK SEAMANSHIP

## COLIN JARMAN

ADLARD COLES LIMITED
**GRANADA PUBLISHING**
London Toronto Sydney New York

Published by Granada Publishing in
Adlard Coles Limited, 1979

Granada Publishing Limited
Frogmore, St Albans, Herts AL2 2NF
and
3 Upper James Street, London W1R 4BP
1221 Avenue of the Americas, New York, NY 10020 USA
117 York Street, Sydney, NSW 2000, Australia
100 Skyway Avenue, Toronto, Ontario, Canada M9W 3A6
Trio City, Coventry Street, Johannesburg 2001, South Africa
CML Centre, Queen and Wyndham, Auckland 1, New Zealand

Copyright © Colin Jarman, 1979

ISBN 0229 11588 8

Printed in Great Britain by
Fletcher & Son Ltd, Norwich

# CONTENTS

For Mary

# INTRODUCTION

As we all have to do some deck work whenever we go sailing this book is not simply a beginner's guide, it is aimed at all levels of experience and competence. It does discuss the most basic on-deck tasks and tends to choose the simplest cases, but the emphasis is on doing each job on deck in a well planned, methodical and safe way. My aim throughout is to make the reader think and plan ahead so that he goes on deck to perform a task knowing exactly what tools or equipment to take with him and in what sequence he will work. In time this will produce faster working, but haste is rarely a safety aid at sea and quickness of working should only come through practise.

For beginners, I hope this book will offer a firm base on which to build skill and experience, for although the methods described may not work every time on every boat, they should establish a reserve of knowledge on which to draw when new situations are met. More experienced yachtsmen may hold different opinions on some subjects, but if they are made to *think* about how they work on deck and whether or not they are performing tasks in the safest, most efficient way, then my purpose will have been served.

The message for all must be 'think safety.'

*Colin Jarman, 1978.*

# ACKNOWLEDGE-MENTS

I am very grateful to Rodney Sutton for his excellent work on drawings 1, 2, 7, 8, 15 and 16. My thanks go also to Mary, my wife, who helped me with the others and either took or acted as model in most of the photographs. For the rest, I would like to thank Andrew Bray of Yachting Monthly for taking photos 4 and 5, and mention that those in photo 8 were taken by Roger M Smith.

# CHAPTER ONE

# DECK DESIGN

Good deck design and layout are basic requirements for the safe, efficient working of any boat. In an emergency essential gear and equipment must come readily to hand, not just by knowing where it is, but by its being in the most easily accessible place. People must be able to concentrate on the job (whatever it may happen to be) without having to remember not to trip over a particular obstruction, or having to stretch for a cleat just beyond arm's reach. It is no use having wide expanses of deck from which you can really swig hard on a halyard, if the positioning of its cleat is so bad that you lose all the tension gained while turning up the fall. In other words there must be careful co-ordination between the requirements of each job both within itself, and in terms of how it affects other work. For example it may be ideal on a particular boat to have an anchor stowed in deck chocks at the foot of the mast when at sea; yet it may not be possible if it is also necessary to stand on that precise spot to work the roller reefing gear. A compromise must be sought.

Most of us buy stock boats on which there is a limit to how much can be changed without major structural alterations. You can't start ripping off decks and cabin tops to replan the deck layout but, by fairly simple re-arrangement of gear and equipment, it should be possible to improve safety and efficiency.

When thinking about how best to lay out the deck, it helps to define the use of each area and so distinguish the requirements for that area. For example, the foredeck is used almost exclusively for setting and handing the headsails, hoisting the mainsail and handling the anchor and its cable or picking up moorings. It should thus be possible to arrange everything on the foredeck so as to help with those jobs – remembering that the layout for one task must not interfere with another.

First take the question of setting and handing headsails. There must be room enough at the forestay for unbagging and hanking on – either from a position just abaft or just forward of the stay. It is more usual to work from abaft the stay, but some people prefer to sit in the pulpit facing aft. This work has to be done either sitting or kneeling, so clearly this is not the place to stow an anchor. Then when the sail is hoisted there must be room to stand at the mast and harden up the halyard using a winch, or to swig it up. If there is room for this there is likely to be room for hoisting the mainsail, but is there space to stand and work the reefing gear?

When a headsail drops on the foredeck it can easily fall on top of some cleat, anchor windlass or other obstruction, hiding it from the deckhand moving about to gather the sail, putting him in danger of tripping over. The sail is also then vulnerable to being torn. Thus it is important to keep as much as possible in the way of cleats, eyebolts, navel pipes and the like out to the sides of the deck. At night too an unwary foot tripping over a badly placed fitting could pitch you overboard, especially if the sea is rough and the boat is leaping about a bit.

The modern trend is away from substantial samson posts set right through the kingplank to the keel, and most boats have a cleat bolted through the deck to a back-up plate which spreads the load. Not all these are either big enough or strong enough, in my opinion, but, be that as it may, why not at least consider having two really good sized cleats set (one each side) out by the toerail? The lead can still be fair from a suitably shaped bow roller or fairlead. They can be big enough to allow the anchor cable to be turned up securely, and they do not lead it close past the forestay deck fitting, which saves a lot of serious chafe. Having such cleats out near the toerails also leaves a little more space towards the middle of the deck.

The navel pipe too can often be better positioned. It is painful to sit down on suddenly when the boat throws you off balance and, provided that the chain will run freely, it does not have to take up valuable working space. It could be placed between the feet of the pulpit on one side, or even ahead of the forestay if there is room. True, it will need plugging with a rag or plasticine in a rough sea, but that is often true wherever it goes on the foredeck. How about close in by the foot of the mast if the mast is forward of the coachroof? Think too about the run of the cable from the navel pipe to the stowed anchor; an unwary foot on that in the dark and you'll quickly be on your back. Keep it short and keep the anchor away from sail handling areas. We will say more about anchor stowage in Chapter 6.

Fairleads deserve consideration for, although they are usually set into the toerail and are thus out of harm's way, they do not always provide a fair lead. That is their whole purpose and it cannot be achieved if they do not, first of all, hold the warp or line in place and, secondly, do not guide it easily toward the required cleat.

Crossover fairleads (that is ones with partly crossed arms) are better than the ones with open jaws, but there must be sufficient gap between the crossed arms to get a line in without using force. Better still are the fully enclosed fairleads, ones that form a complete circle, since these by nature hold the line no matter what angle it makes with the fairlead; open fairleads will release the line if there is any upward pull on it.

The fairleads must be placed carefully to ensure they can give the required clean lead. If they are too far in from the side of the boat, a line leading upward to them can chafe against the rubbing strake and wear that away or, if they are set so that a line leads from them to the cleat but rubs against the foot of a pulpit leg, that too is no good. The very fittings themselves must be chosen with care as it has been noticeable in recent years that cleats and fairleads are being marketed that have been designed to look good rather than to perform well. Some of them are smart polished alloy of jazzy shape, but clearly the designer wasn't told that sharp edges, or even just hard angled edges, will chafe a rope badly.

Square in the middle of the foredeck there is often a forehatch, and as it is important to have one, and as there is almost nowhere else to put it, there is little to be said about it. Forehatches are big enough and should be strong enough to form a slightly raised part of the foredeck working area and they should be treated accordingly. They must be waterproof and as non-slip as the rest of the working areas (see next section). If the coachroof extends well in front of the mast, the hatch can be set in the forward end to keep the deck clear, but it must not interfere with work at the mast.

Movement forward to the foredeck or aft to the cockpit is by way of either the

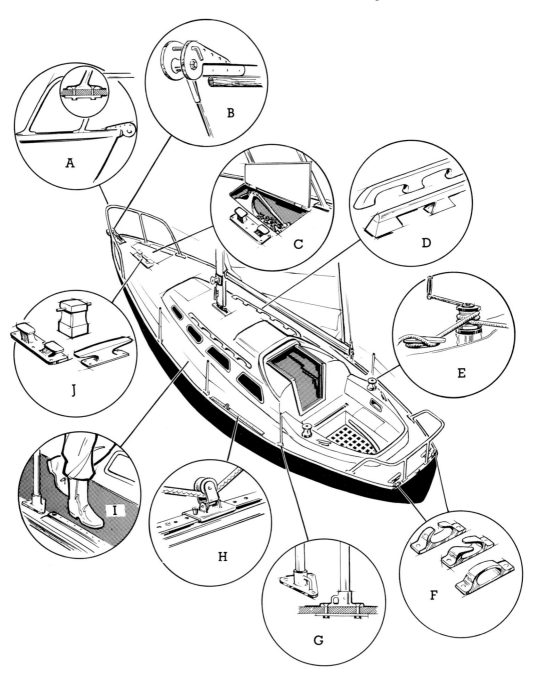

sidedecks or the coachroof. The coachroof is also used for standing on to hand and stow the mainsail, and possibly for reefing it. There are normally grabrails running fore and aft along the length of the coachroof but, if a dinghy is stowed here, it may cover them. I'll say more about that later on.

The larger the boat the more likely you are to use the sidedecks for moving forward or aft. With a small boat, say one of about 6 metres (18-20 ft), the side decks are usually too narrow for easy walking, so most people clamber over the cabin top. This puts them in a dangerous

FIG. 1
Basic ideas for safer deck design. A, strong pulpit with feet bolted through the deck to back up pads. B, high cheeked bow roller that carries the anchor cable well ahead of the stem and has a pin through the cheeks to prevent the cable jumping out. C, anchor stowed in a well keeps the deck clear. D, strong grabrails bolted through the deck and affording a really secure hold. E, easy working area round winch ; *never* leave a handle in a winch. F, normal, better and best fairleads : a warp can jump out of the normal fairlead while it is harder from the 'cross over' type and impossible from the enclosed lifeboat ones. G, guardrail stanchions fitted in strong sockets securely bolted through the deck to back up plates. H, sheet track and foot block close to toerail presents minimum obstruction on sidedecks. I, wide sidedecks with an effective non-slip surface. J, mooring bitts : samson post with staghorn, cleat and double headed bollard. The samson post or bollard is to be preferred, but whatever is used must be big enough to hold the cable easily, and be very strong and secure.

position without any real handholds, but it is a toss up between that and the slow awkwardness of shuffling along the sidedecks. Where a boat has built-up topsides (a full width cabin top) there is of course no choice but to go over the coachroof.

Headsail sheet fairleads and tracks are the commonest obstructions placed on sidedecks, though if an alloy extrusion is used for the toerail, this can carry the fairleads thus leaving the deck clear. While it is part of the designer's job to keep the sidedecks as clear as possible, if he puts a track and fairleads down the middle, you would be unwise to move the leads out to the toerail as the sails will have been made to sheet down to the designed position. What you can do however is to keep the length of track used to a minimum and place any cleats that are needed out at the toerail.

The final deck working area, other than the cockpit, which is dealt with later in this chapter, is the after deck. As a working area at sea, the after deck is little used, it really comes into its own as a warp handling platform when berthing. The cleats and fairleads on each quarter must be arranged to work in unison, the fairlead guiding the warp easily to the cleat and the cleat accepting it at the correct angle. As with the foredeck fairleads, the quarter ones are best if fully enclosed so that they always work no matter how the boat may rise and fall. It is rare now to see quarter posts in the cockpit. They have been replaced by cleats on the after deck, but these are not always big enough, nor are they given sufficient space to allow a heavy line to be made up properly. Don't place them too close to the toerail or the feet of the pushpit.

## Deck surfaces and coverings

Glassfibre boats normally have glassfibre decks and these usually have an integral diamond pattern which is supposed to be non-slip. In fact at best it reduces the chances of slipping, and then only if you have good deck shoes or boots. It is far better than a smooth surface or one with a so-called 'leather' finish, but even this is not ideal.

The point of any deck covering or finish, apart from protecting the deck and stopping it leaking, is to give a good grip to the feet. To do this the surface has to be rough and unfortunately that usually makes it abrasive to clothing and bare skin.

To achieve non-slip one can use paint with sand mixed into it (or some proprietory paint-on surfacing), the integral diamond pattern mentioned before, adhesive surfacings, or laid wooden planks (usually teak). Each has its advantages and disadvantages: paint is cheap but needs re-coating frequently, at least once a season; a diamond pattern is permanent, but it is not all that non-slip and it is hard to keep clean; adhesive surfacings can be put on over any deck be it wood, plastic or metal, but some are much better than others; laid teak decks are certainly the most attractive in appearance and are both efficient and extremely hard wearing, but they are expensive, mark easily and are relatively heavy.

In my opinion the best surfaces are either laid teak, if you can stand the expense and don't need to worry about the weight, or an adhesive surfacing called *Treadmaster M*. This is made in sheets of large raised diamonds and is widely used on such craft as life-boats. A close rival to these is a surface called *She Deck* which has the appearance of a laid deck, but is in fact a synthetic composite. It is not widely used as it involves skilled work and is a bit slow to produce, but it is good.

The need for good non-slip working surfaces is paramount if the crew is going to be able to perform their appointed tasks in reasonable safety. They cannot be expected to work well if they are constantly slipping about in danger of going over the side, and to this end it is most important to ensure that *all* working surfaces are covered with a non-skid surfacing. On any boat there are hatches, sloping coach-coamings and other such places that are not designed to be trodden on, but in fact are. Each of these must be indentified and covered with a non-slip material. Strips of one of the adhesive surfacings are all that is needed, but as soon as you find yourself stepping on an area of smooth plastic, varnished or painted wood, note it and apply a strip of the material as soon as possible. If you do not, there will be an accident – probably a minor one, but it could be serious, such as a man slipping overboard.

## Hatches

There will be at least two hatches on a boat – the mainhatch and the forehatch – and possibly a number more. Each of these must be strong enough to stand on and must have a non-slip surface. This latter point is all too often ignored, creating a large, dangerously slippery area when the decks are wet. Apart from their obvious uses for access and ventilation, the hatches can form secure working stations. For instance on a small boat it may be possible to hoist sails or handle the anchor from the safety of the forehatch, while the main hatch provides the navigator with a secure place in which to stand and take a series of compass bearings.

The forehatch is very frequently used when changing headsails as it avoids the necessity of dragging heavy, clumsy bags along the deck and through the accommodation. It is perhaps when moving forward or aft along the deck, particularly with one or two hands full of sailbag, that a crewman is at greatest risk during sail changing operations, so anything to reduce the number of trips is to be encouraged.

If the forehatch is to be used for access to sails stowed in the forepeak, it will help if the hatch can be opened and closed from on deck. Some of the modern acrylic or toughened glass translucent hatches are made with handles that can be worked from outside and, although they create a slight hazard in that you can stub your toes and trip over the handles or snag a sail on them, I think they are worthwhile if well placed and designed. The other thing to watch if sails are to be pushed through a hatchway is that there are no sharp projections around the coaming that might tear the sail.

## Toerails

Recent years have seen great changes in yacht toerails with extrusions of one type or another becoming increasingly common, and the older wooden toerail slowly being pushed out of use on modern production boats. While the basic function of the toerail (to mark the edge of the deck and afford a final foot bracing point) remains unchanged, the use of alloy extrusions has given them added purpose. Now the rail can act as a securing point for lead blocks, guys, braces, downhauls, vangs, and can carry headsail sheet fairleads, giving them infinite variation of position fore and aft. These additional functions are made possible by the toerail having regularly spaced holes along its whole length, and its upper surface being shaped to act as a track for sliding sheet fairleads.

Some of these toerails can incorporate cleats and fairleads for mooring lines, thus moving these obstructions right to the edge of any working area. Guardrail stanchion bases too can be incorporated in the toerail.

## Guardrails

The purpose of guardrails and their supporting stanchions is to keep you safely on board. They must therefore be strong enough to withstand a man's full weight being thrown at them, and they must be of a height that will not trip him up. In this regard the general rule for the height of guardrails is that they should be no lower than 0.6 metres (2ft) unless there is some real, unalterable restriction. That is the minimum height, and many would argue that about 0.75 metres (30in) is better. Their argument is that as a boat heels, so the leeward rails go down and you (relatively) go up, thus reducing the effective height of the rails.

If a person really is thrown against the guardrails or a stanchion, a tremendous force is exerted which tries to wrench the stanchion base out of the deck. It needs to be bolted down through the deck to substantial back-up plates to withstand this force and, if possible, it should also be secured to the toerail or a bulwark where one exists.

Some people use only one guardwire at the top of the stanchions, but it is wise to have an intermediate one as well. The reason for this is that it is quite possible for a person to be swept off his feet or to be caught off balance and roll under a single wire, but he is unlikely to go under a middle one.

The guardrails should be connected at the bows to a pulpit and at the stern to a pushpit, thus completely enclosing the decks. To stop the rails at the forward end of the cockpit is to leave yourself unguarded in an area that is surprisingly dangerous, and from which many people have been lost. Imagine working a sheet winch when the boat takes a sudden roll to leeward. What have you to grab at as you are pitched over the side? Not a lot if there is no guardrail handy.

Whether the guardrails should be of rope, stainless steel wire, or galvanized wire coated in plastic is a matter of personal choice. The rope must create a certain amount of windage if it is of sufficiently large diameter to be strong, but it is then large enough to give a good, comfortable handhold. It's also fairly cheap to buy and easy to put eyesplices in its ends to secure it to pulpit and pushpit. Stainless wire is the most commonly used material, followed by plastic coated galvanized wire. If the latter is being used, make sure the coating is cut off where the swageing ferrule is put on when forming the eyes at each end; if this is not done the swage can slip. The stanchions themselves are usually either stainless steel or alloy, though a few people use galvanized tubing. If the guardwires and stanchions are of different metals they must be insulated from each other at each meeting point to avoid any galvanic action; it will also cut down chafe.

Few boats have no pulpit as it makes working on a pitching foredeck so much safer, but not everyone agrees about the need for a pushpit. I think it is very desirable to have one as it completes the all round fence, and it keeps the guardrails high as they pass the cockpit. This does mean however that the mainsheet can chafe on the top wire when it is run off. This problem can be alleviated by a length of plastic tube threaded onto the wire to act as a roller (but if it is loose enough to roll freely, the security of a handhold is reduced at that point). A better system is to have a mainsheet horse across the stern at the height of the top rail. This is not often done but it works excellently.

The ends of the guardrails should never be secured to the pulpit or pushpit with either shackles or turnbuckles as it is impossible to undo either of these instantly in an emergency. It may be necessary to drop the guardrails to recover a man from the water, and that is no time to fiddle about with shackle spanners or spikes and locknuts. The ends should either be secured with rope lashings which can be cut, or with pelican hooks which can be slipped and opened quickly; these must be kept greased to ensure easy working. Don't be fooled by the argument that lashings don't keep the rails bar taut – they can (but the rails don't, in fact, need to be; they should be just taut enough not to give too much when leant on). If insulators are used to break the magnetic loop which interferes with DF sets, they should be of the type that leaves the rails joined even if the insulators fail. In other words the ends of the guardwires should interlock round the insulators.

Canvas spray dodgers rigged on the guardrails by the cockpit are a mixed blessing as they obscure vision and create windage, but they do give some protection and can help in preventing children from falling overboard.

**Grabrails**

As their name implies, grabrails are meant to be grabbed. They must provide an instant, absolutely secure handhold from as wide a variety of directions as possible. If you grab from one angle and are then hurled round to a completely different angle, your hold should still be safe. It is common to find coachroof grabrails set too close to the cabin top, so that you are forced to release your grip when pitched across them as your knuckles are jammed between rail and cabin top. Some coachroof grabrails are simply pieces of wood curved over without any finger holes. These are very bad indeed as a fingertip hold will not support any weight – you *must* be able to get your hand right round the rail.

A good addition to the conventional coachroof grabrails are lines stretched from the after end of the cabin top to the mast, being secured there at about gooseneck height. Not only can a lifeharness be clipped onto them for moving from cockpit to mast, but they are that much higher than the other grabrails and so one is less likely to be pitched over them when the boat rolls suddenly.

If a rigid dinghy is carried on deck and it covers the coachroof grabrails, the runners on the bottom of the dinghy should be enlarged to form adequate substitutes, otherwise lines must be rigged fore and aft to act as grabrails. This is also likely to be required when a part-inflated rubber dinghy is carried.

It is not only on the coachroof that grabrails are required. There should be good ones either side of the companionway, as you are particularly vulnerable and likely to be caught off balance when stepping into or out of the cabin. Although we are only concerned here with safety above decks, let me say that it is almost impossible to have too many grab points on a boat, either above or below decks, but it is amazing how many boats do not even have a bare minimum; particularly in the cabin. If you are looking at a new boat, try to imagine her pitching and tossing about. Is there a secure handhold for you everywhere you go? Is it where you instinctively put your hand? If not you'll always be slightly off balance as you reach for support.

A handhold may be built in, in the form of grabrails, guardrails, pulpit and pushpit, or it may be inherent in the form of shrouds, mast or cockpit coaming. Whatever it is there must be no doubt at all as to its integrity. A weak handhold is worse than none at all. Go round the boat and study what you hold on to; watch others and note what they use. Then make certain that all grabpoints are strong. Attached grabrails must be through-bolted and back-up plates must be used to spread the loads. These handholds are less obvious safety aids than lifebuoys, liferafts and the rest, but are just as important since their job is to prevent some of the other safety aids being used.

## Footwear

Shoes or boots that give a good grip, even on wet surfaces, are a great boon when working on deck. There are many makes of shoes and boots specially designed for use afloat, each having some form of patterned tread that is reluctant to slip on any surface other than smooth paint and varnish or unroughened plastic. An annoying habit of many of these soles is that they pick up dirt and grit if worn ashore so that, if they are not washed off before stepping back aboard, the grit will scuff and scar the boat besides making everything dirty.

Unfortunately, specialized boating footwear is not cheap, but you do need one pair of shoes and one pair of boots. The boots should be large enough to put on over at least one pair of thick socks,

preferably two, and should be easily removable in the event of falling overboard when they can seriously impede swimming. Knee length boots are better than short ones in that they can be used to walk in deeper water before they fill up, and also there is less chance of a gap between oilskin trouser bottoms and boot tops when kneeling down to work on deck, but they are harder to get on and off. Not unnaturally they also cost more than short boots.

## Lifeharnesses

There must be a lifeharness on board for every member of the crew, who must accustom themselves to using them. As with all items of boating gear and equipment, there is a bewildering number of makes of harness available and selection needs careful thought. They must be easy to put on over foul weather gear, even when the boat is tossing around wildly and room below is cramped. They must obviously be strongly constructed with a stout snaphook and line. They must be comfortable to wear and easily adjustable to fit snugly, and the shoulder straps must keep the belt well up on the chest. Incorporating a harness in either a lifejacket or an oilskin jacket is of questionable value, but the latter is the better arrangement. I prefer a separate harness because it is then designed specifically for the job of keeping you on board (or at least attached to the boat), without any other considerations.

There is a British Standard for lifeharnesses, but only one maker has yet managed to find the large sum of money required to have their products continuously tested to qualify for the Kitemark symbol. Some lifeharnesses do conform to the specifications laid down in the British Standard, but for the most part it is left to the purchaser to decide whether or not he likes the design and considers the whole thing strong enough. Amongst the best available are those made by Peter Haward who pioneered the design and use of lifeharnesses. I find his Waistcoat harness particularly good as the belt is supported by a bright orange waistcoat that can be seen easily and eliminates shoulder straps that are hard to untangle in a hurry. A large spring hook at the end of the safety line is used to hook on with, but a smaller hook half way along the line can be used either to shorten the line's scope (for instance you can lean back against it when both hands are needed for a job), and in very bad conditions it can be used to hook onto a secure point while the end hook is transferred to a new strong point, thus avoiding a period when you are not hooked on.

Any harness must be strong in itself, but the object it is hooked onto must also be completely secure. For ease of movement fore and aft along the deck, a jackstay (a strong rope or wire) stretched loosely along the sidedeck from bow to stern is ideal. A crewman can clip onto this at the cockpit and then slide his lifeharness hook along it as he moves forward. When he gets to the foredeck he can do all his work without unclipping from the jackstay and can then return to the cockpit still attached. If two people need to pass each other then one of course has to unclip, but otherwise this is a good arrangement.

The helmsman can also clip onto this jackstay, using the windward one, just in case he is thrown across the cockpit by a bad sea, but it is worth considering a pair of lines in the foot well. These can run along the inboard sides of the cockpit lockers for the exclusive use of people in the cockpit, thus leaving the deck jackstays free for people moving about on deck. Similar lines can also be run vertically on each side of the companionway to give anyone coming up from below an immediate point to clip on to before ever leaving the cabin.

Fixed metal eyes should not be used as clip on points since they can trip normal snap hooks open, but a British manufacturer, M S Gibb, does now make specially designed non-trippable snaphooks and also eyes that will not trip conventional snaphooks open. I still think the safer system is to use jackstays, but if preferred a fixed eye can be fitted and a soft wire or rope grommet worked into it. This grommet can twist with the hook thus avoiding accidents.

When should a lifeharness be worn? This is a tricky question to answer. Perhaps the best way is to say that a harness should *not* be worn in fog, because of the risk of being unable to detach yourself from the boat if by some terrible mischance you are run down. No one wears a harness all the time, but people will be encouraged to wear them if they are easy to put on, easy to work in, and there are readily available clip on points. A person on watch alone at night or in bad weather should definitely wear a harness, so should anyone working on deck in rough going, but to insist that people wear them on calm sunny days is impracticable. Children may be an exception to this.

## Lifejackets

Lifejackets should be worn in preference to lifeharnesses in fog, but at other times they are of less value on a ballasted keel boat than they are in a dinghy. It is sensible to wear one going ashore in the tender, or on board if you cannot swim and are not wearing a lifeharness, but otherwise I think the harness is preferable as it tends to keep you on board. Should you choose to wear both at the same time, be very careful that neither interferes with the operation of the other. In some cases it is an insurance requirement that lifejackets are carried.

## Lifebuoy stowage

There must be no delay in throwing a lifebuoy to a person in the water, so they must be stowed securely but without anything holding them that cannot be released instantly. The commonest solution with a horseshoe lifebuoy is to put its legs into a canvas pocket attached to the cockpit dodgers or to the guardrails. These pockets hold the two legs of the buoy securely, yet the buoy can be lifted straight out and thrown overboard.

A system which can also be used with a ring-shaped lifebuoy, is to have loops of shockcord over the buoy, held with greased pegs; the pegs are slipped and the buoy is free to be thrown. Alternatively a single piece of shockcord can be stretched right across the buoy allowing it to be lifted out. This is a good method for a buoy stowed flat on either the mainhatch or the after deck.

If a flashing light is attached to the lifebuoy this must be held upside down in a clip beside the lifebuoy; it can then be unclipped and hurled over with the buoy. These lights are generally activated by turning the right way up, though a few have seawater activated switches.

## Liferafts and their stowage

It is essential when only one liferaft is carried that it is big enough to take the whole crew, and it must have an up to date inspection certificate. For family cruisers we are talking really about 4 or 6 man liferafts either packed in soft valises or hard plastic canisters. They must be serviced regularly by an approved service agent so as to keep them in proper working order. It would be a terrible situation if you launched the liferaft and found it did not inflate or, if it inflated, that it subsequently collapsed because of a puncture.

Makers' instructions will differ from raft to raft, but generally a painter is secured to a strong point on the boat, the raft is thrown overboard, and the painter is pulled until it triggers the inflation system. The raft then inflates and can be entered by the abandoning crew. Every person on board must be familiar with the operating instructions and with the method of releasing the liferaft from its stowage.

The majority of liferafts packed in hard canisters are stowed on deck somewhere, while the ones packed in a soft valise are usually placed in a locker for protection. In any stowage situation the liferaft must be protected from damage by seas, weather, and people standing on it, either by virtue of its own canister or the locker it is stowed in, and it must be readily moved to the vessel's side and launched. This latter consideration causes problems because clearly the liferaft must not impede the everyday working of the ship.

A lot of people place their liferafts on the cabin top near the mast where, although it is vulnerable to any sea coming aboard and is liable to be trodden on, it is immediately accessible. Another place often chosen is in the pushpit, but here it can be a nuisance when handling docking lines. Both of these stowages involve quick-release devices for retaining the raft in its chocks, and these normally take the form of straps with either pelican hooks at one end or lashings that can be cut.

When a raft is stowed in a locker, usually in the cockpit or after deck, it must be remembered that the conditions may be very rough when it has to be heaved out and got to the rail. Liferafts are no light weight, even the 4-man ones. Do you think a *weak* member of your crew could manage it? It may not be the strongest person on board who has to launch the raft; that person may be injured. For that matter it is not going to be easy, even in a calm sea, to launch the raft from the cabin top. Some people argue that in a dire emergency you will find the strength. I don't know, and if it comes to that, I'm not too keen to find out.

One suggested stowage is in the foot well of the cockpit on a grating to keep it out of any water and under a cover that can be stepped on. That way it is readily available but it's also well protected.

With a multihull there is the added possibility of needing to launch the liferaft after the vessel has capsized. When the boat is upside down it is no use expecting to be able to dive down and release the raft from the deck or a deck locker, it must be reached either through a removable hatch in the bottom of a hull or float, or better still from a stowage on the after face of a crossbeam. If the raft is stowed on the outside of a crossbeam it is easy to launch with the boat either way up; the holding straps are cast off and the raft drops off–one way or the other.

Whatever your final decision on liferaft stowage it is vital to think it out carefully. The idea of stowing the raft outboard on a multihull gives rise to the thought that a designer could usefully design a stowage for a solid canister into the transom of a monohull. It would not interfere with the working of the boat and would be easy to launch as no lifting would be required.

## Siting winches

A sheet winch must be angled to accept the sheet directly from the lead block, and it must be placed so that the person working the winch can do so to the best advantage with the least difficulty. These are the two basic requirements when siting a sheet winch, but there are others, such as avoiding obstructing sidedecks or other working areas, proximity to other winches in a 'farm', and the possibility of cutting down the total number of winches needed by using one for several jobs.

If you buy a stock family cruiser you are likely to find she has a couple of halyard winches (on the mast), a pair of genoa winches (one on each cockpit coaming), and possibly a pair of smaller spinnaker sheet/guy winches (also on the cockpit coaming). To save money, the builder will in all probability fit the smallest winch that'll do the job, yet a winch one size larger (on a medium size of boat) does not cost a great deal more, and it may be worth spending the money when buying a new boat to ensure that the weaker crew members will be able to handle the sails easily. It's demoralizing not to be able to grind in the largest genoa, and making the job less physically demanding with a larger winch saves energy and so promotes safety.

Winches need careful siting otherwise silly things happen, such as their handles fouling the guardrails or dodgers; easily avoidable but quite common. The same with bottom action winches where the handles remain in place; they are often mounted on pedestals outside the cockpit coaming – but not quite far enough outside and the handles constantly dig into the back of anyone sitting by them. Too often they are mounted on extensions of the cockpit coamings which are smooth and shiny, giving no grip to knees or feet. These too are extremely dangerous areas to step on when climbing out of the cockpit. They must be angled properly for a fair lead in to the barrel, else there will be snarl-ups and riding turns that can be devils to undo. Cleats must be on the opposite side of the winch to the lead-in of the sheet, otherwise all the loads are trying to uproot the winch.

### Cockpit design

Here again if you buy a stock boat you are more or less stuck with what you've got, but your choice may be influenced by just that – what you get. The cockpit is the place you do a large part of your sailing from, so it must be comfortable and practical.

There must be good all round vision from the helm if the helmsman is going to stand watches alone. There will almost certainly be some blind areas, created by a dinghy stowed on deck, or a low cut genoa, but these areas must be made as small as possible (and ideally eliminated) for, when the helmsman is alone on watch, he cannot keep leaving the tiller to take a look round. Make sure that it is possible at the very least to see over the cabin top without standing up.

Unless the tiller is at a comfortable height, or the wheel has a comfortable seat by it, a long watch can be very demanding. It helps too when tacking with several people in the cockpit if the tiller can be lifted as the boat is put about. The helmsman can then slide across to the other bench without bumping into everyone.

The mainsheet should be conveniently placed as the helmsman is the likeliest person to have to handle it. Double ended mainsheets make this easy if the mainsail is sheeted down to a horse across the after deck, as there is then a fall by the helmsman on either tack. With a mainsheet coming down to a horse athwartships between the cockpit benches, the helmsman is enclosed in what amounts to a separate cockpit, which can make it difficult for him to handle the genoa sheets if he's on his own. It does help enormously if he can trim these sheets from the tiller, as he can then maintain a steady course while doing it.

The steering compass and other sailing instruments need to be sited so that they are easily read from the helm, and in the case of the compass it is essential that there are no problems with parallax on either tack. The helmsman must be able to look as nearly straight at it as possible from both sides of the boat, otherwise there may be a difference of several degrees between the actual course and the course read from one side or the other. To avoid this problem some boats have twin steering compasses mounted one each side of the cockpit, but this means having two deviation cards, thus giving the navigator added problems. A guard for the compass is sometimes needed to prevent lines wrapping round it or people stepping or leaning on it. A cage can be built over it using plastic, stainless steel, or bronze (non-ferrous materials).

Sailing instruments are most often built into the after edge of the hatch garage so that they can be seen by anyone in the cockpit. Big racing boats may have repeaters dotted all over the boat, but for simpler craft this is the easiest position.

Engine controls must be within easy reach of the helmsman, and they can often be conveniently recessed into the side of a cockpit locker; recess must be complete, however, as it is easy to wrap sheets round them or to catch trouser legs on them.

Ideally it should be possible to gain access to cockpit lockers without disturbing the helmsman, but on most boats he will have to be shifted because the lids usually form the cockpit seats, and you can guarantee that he has just settled down on the one you want to get at.

As the cockpit is the place the boat is really worked from, there should be room for the whole crew and still allow the boat to be sailed. That's a tall order when you look at the number of berths modern boats have, but there should at least be sitting space for everyone. Cockpit cushions make life more comfortable, and if made so that they float they can double as extra lifebuoys if someone goes over the side; rope loops round their edges make them easier to grab hold of.

If the cockpit well is self-draining the drains must be big (at least $1\frac{1}{2}$ in internal diameter) and without grilles over them, for although these may prevent objects falling down the pipes, they greatly reduce the draining rate. Perhaps a compromise is acceptable using large grilles rather than fine household sink ones. The most effective cockpit drains are large bore holes straight out through the transom, with non-return flaps on the outside.

Not all cockpits are self-draining, though most modern boats have them, and if they are not they must be kept small. In some ways they are safer than self-draining ones as they can be deeper. A self-draining well is of necessity quite shallow as its sole must be above the waterline.

Apart from the lockers under the cockpit seats, one or two open-fronted cave lockers in the coamings are handy for keeping winch handles and sail tiers in at sea; odd bits of cordage or even coffee mugs can also be put out of the way in them.

Cockpit locker lids must be made as nearly watertight as possible, not just to keep the rain out (which should in any case be channelled into the footwell by built-in drains), but to keep out a sea should the boat be pooped. If they are not watertight then they will fill and hold the stern down, seriously affecting the boat's ability to lift to the next sea. To this end also there should be a strong bridgedeck of at least locker-top height between the well and the cabin, but this is all too often omitted on today's boats. I agree that few boats in the course of the average family's summer sailing are ever boarded by a green sea – but it only needs to happen once for an ill-prepared boat to be in serious trouble. For the same reason there should be a large capacity bilge pump operable from the cockpit with the cabin and all lockers secured shut. There should also be one down below if you are going on an offshore cruise.

There must be adequate lifeharness attachment points in and about the cockpit as discussed earlier, and the sole and sidebenches should be covered with a non-slip surface, or wooden slats if that is considered more comfortable. The lifebuoy and any other man overboard aids should all be within easy reach of the helmsman.

I have stressed several safety aspects of the cockpit arrangement as it is a surprisingly dangerous place. Just because you are surrounded by a coaming and you can sit down in a normal fashion with your feet well below your knees, you tend to be lulled into a false sense of security. An unfortunate number of people have been lost from cockpits. Not just washed out in heavy weather, but by falling out through forgetting to take a good handhold, or overbalancing when working a leeward sheet winch. Beware.

CHAPTER TWO

# MOVING ABOUT ON DECK

As soon as a boat is anchored, swinging to a mooring, or berthed in a marina, we tend to become lax about moving safely and carefully round the deck. We all walk about upright (a natural land posture, but not one suited to an unpredictably moving boat), using few real handholds. We may grab a shroud in passing or rest a hand on the mast, but it is quite likely that we will hold onto something as flimsy as a signal halyard; something that would give no support at all if the boat were rolling along in a seaway. For some reason we suddenly lose (or at least relax) our powers of discrimination. In other words we put ourselves in danger.

This ability to discriminate between safe hand or foot holds and temporary ones is essential to safe deckwork. Imagine if someone pushes you in the back. You put your foot out to stop yourself falling forwards and, if you are standing by the shrouds at the time, you'll probably grab at them as well. You instinctively try to save yourself by grabbing or pushing against some object, but what happens if you are prancing about out of reach of such an object when you lose your balance?

In many ways you are probably in greater danger when moving about on deck in quite calm conditions than you are doing the same things in rough weather. Under the calm conditions you can so easily be caught off guard, while in the heavy stuff you are probably attached with a lifeharness and may be on your hands and knees, but in any case you will be aware of the boat's motion and on the lookout for abnormal lurches. Let's look at the danger areas on deck.

I've already mentioned that the cockpit is not as completely safe as most people believe it to be, but getting into or out of the cockpit are certainly danger times. Whether coming up from below or stepping up onto the sidedecks or coachroof, you are standing very high with often little to hold onto. For this reason it is essential to have grabhandles by the companionway, and to use both the coachroof grabrails and the guardwires when stepping over the cockpit coaming. Always work your way forward on the windward side unless there is some very good reason for going down to leeward. Move deliberately from handhold to handhold until it becomes instinctive (even then you *should* still do it consciously). This of course is difficult if you are lugging a big sail bag with you, but if you really have to take it with you rather than fetch it up through a forehatch, move slowly and carefully, making sure you are always braced against something. If it comes to the crunch, save yourself and let the sailbag go.

Once you reach the foredeck, there is often more distance than the spread of your outstretched arms between the mast and the forestay. In this case you either make a lurching dive from one to the other, or you take the more sensible course of going round via the guardrails. How many people actually do it though? Yes, I've been guilty too.

One solution to this problem of too much space between foredeck handholds is to rig a strong line from the mast (say a spinnaker pole attachment, or even the hounds) down to an eye or mooring cleat. This line serves the double function of offering a half way hold and preventing the headsail sheets snagging on mast cleats and belayed halyard falls when tacking.

A lot of sail handling puts a crewman in danger because he has to use both hands for the job rather than holding on with one and working with the other. He is particularly vulnerable when the work involves standing up and reaching out near the guardrails. Moving a spinnaker pole about on deck, and certainly when fixing it onto the mast, are good examples of this. One man can handle a 3 metre (10ft) pole in terms of its weight, but lifting it, timing the boat's roll, and inserting it into a mast cup or clipping it onto a ring is no joke. He is standing up, carrying a heavy, unwieldy object, with no handhold, and almost nothing to brace against. That's a dangerous time.

Reaching out to the mainboom end to unwrap a topping lift from the backstay is another common sight; man standing on afterdeck or cockpit bench, both arms upward, body slanted out across the lee guardrails. One lurch and there is *nothing* to stop him going in the water. If he is the skipper and his crew are his wife and children, are they going to manage to pick him up? I'm not dealing with how to pick up a man overboard here, but it's a chilling thought.

## Sitting and kneeling

Obviously deckwork need not be a death defying show, but you do have to realize the dangers and go carefully. You must never be ashamed of doing something that promotes your own, the boat's, or another person's safety. An example of this is sitting or kneeling on deck to work, again particularly when handling sails on a wet foredeck. I sailed once with a man who would not be seen doing such things – he felt he would be laughed at, that he would look stupid. It took a slide across the deck and a leg trailing in the bow wave to convince him that he would look a whole lot sillier if he *didn't* get his weight down nearer the deck

Frankly on a small boat it is very much easier, apart from anything else, to work from a sitting or kneeling position. Take as an example handing a large genoa. The halyard is checked away and down

come billowing clouds of canvas. Unless you can smother them the wind will pick the lot up and play merry hell. Sitting on the deck you can fist the whole lot down into your lap and keep it tidy until it can be put into a sailbag or down the forehatch.

In heavy weather, of course, your only safe means of progress forward along the sidedecks may very well be on your hands and knees, or shuffling sideways along the coachroof in a sitting position. Again, no one's laughing. On small boats I have often sat with my legs wrapped round the mast while casting off a halyard or making one up, and certainly when I've not yet acquired my sealegs at the start of a passage I find it the only safe position.

If you consider how much higher the guardrails look (and indeed are, relatively speaking) from a kneeling position it makes sense to keep low down. It cuts down windage too!

## Handling lifeharnesses

They say that practice makes perfect, and it is true enough with respect to coping with a lifeharness while moving about and working on deck. It is fine when you are sitting still at the helm, but it soon snags up and gets in the way when you move about. I've sometimes wondered if a mouse would have the same trouble.

After all they must be used to remembering their tails, and that's about what handling a lifeharness amounts to.

If a jackstay is fitted along the sidedecks, you can clip onto it at the cockpit and work your way forward, with the lifeharness line held just taut in one hand. Like this the hook will slide along the jackstay and the line will not snag on anything. If it is simply allowed to drag along the deck behind you it will almost certainly snag somewhere. In bad conditions, when both hands are needed for support, the line has to be allowed to drag, but keep an eye on it.

Where no jackstays are fitted you have to move from handhold to handhold, unclipping and moving the hook from one secure point to the next; not easy in rough conditions. Between unhooking at one point and clipping on at the next you must be aware of the fact that you are attached to the boat only by the grip of one hand. In other words you are no more secure than the strength of your own grip. This is where a second hook attached half way along the lifeline is a help. Although it cannot be attached to the line as strongly as the one at the end (it is normally seized on, whereas the end hook is held with an eyesplice), nor is it as big as the end hook, it is nevertheless strong enough to hold you against normal boat lurches while you unfasten the final hook and clip it onto the next point.

Certainly it is stronger than a hand's grip. In this way you are never completely unclipped from the boat and are making proper use of the lifeharness.

Once you have reached the mast, foredeck or wherever you were heading for, you should not have to unclip from a jackstay to perform your task. It may be necessary, if for instance you have to go right across to the lee rail on a beamy boat, when you must use the hook-over-hook method (just described) if possible. Failing that you are back to holding on tightly with one hand while moving the hook with the other.

Yes, it can be a slow and fiddly way of moving about but, when you are just disappearing over the side, it is a pretty poor argument to say that you intended hooking on when you got to the mast, or that you only let go for a moment. Surely it's better to use this method and arrange convenient hooking points or jackstays fore and aft with an additional one athwartships by the mast, if need be, to reach both rails? That way you stay safe and, as you become accustomed to it, you will move about quite quickly.

When actually working, that half-way hook can come into its own again. For jobs needing two hands it is sometimes convenient to clip the half-way hook onto the harness and lean back on the short length of line between it and the big end hook. This way you are braced against the line and have both hands free. Except while transferring the end hook from one point to the next, *never* rely solely on the half-way hook, always aim to have the main hook attached.

One problem I at least suffer from quite often is turning round and winding myself up in the lifeline. You have to remember if you turn one way, to unwind the opposite way. Another more general trouble is getting the line tangled up with winch handles. This needs a lot of practice to avoid.

## Handholds and foot braces

Only about one handhold used in eight would actually stop you falling if your whole weight were suddenly thrown onto it. For most of the time when moving about on a boat we use balance retaining holds, which are not expected to bear our full weight but to provide steadying holds, perhaps bridging a gap between fall-averting holds. As you become more accustomed to a particular boat you may find yourself making greater use of these balance retaining holds and braces, relying on a developed sense of balance and awareness of that particular boat's *normal* movements and motion. Which of course leaves you wide open to unexpected lurches.

True fall-averting handholds need to be able to withstand the full weight of a person thrown against them. While they are often ready made (for instance shrouds offer a good hold when of fairly large diameter) most fall-averting handholds are grabrails or handles through-bolted and both large enough in diameter and raised high enough off a surface to provide a really solid grip. This puts the onus on the designer and builder to fit them in the right places and of adequate strength.

Much of the time when working it is impossible (or certainly very hard) to follow the 'one hand for yourself, one for the ship' maxim, and we have to make use of foot and leg braces. For example when working a headsail sheet winch, one hand is used to grind the handle round while the other maintains tension on the tail of the sheet. This leaves only your legs and feet to keep you secure. The same applies when using both hands on the tiller; then you have to brace your feet across the cockpit well against the opposite sidebench.

One thing you have to be very careful of is a false handhold such as a signal halyard or loose halyard fall. Such frail lines could not possibly provide any real support so they should be identified and avoided, or better still, moved to a place where there is no temptation to use them.

Finally there are the taboo handholds, ones that must not be used at all. These include such things as the steering compass and lifebuoys mounted on dodgers. They are dangerous to hold onto, both for you and the boat.

We require and use handholds and foot or leg braces all the time. They must be provided in the right places and they must be strong enough for the job. It is a worthwhile exercise watching other crew members moving about the boat to see how and where they hold on. If people unaccustomed to the boat automatically reach for a hold where there is none, it should be a reminder to the owner to provide one. As soon as people get used to reaching for a hold in a slightly awkward position, or at full stretch, they will cease to notice being off balance and will go on using the hold despite its being dangerous.

CHAPTER THREE
# RUNNING RIGGING

## HALYARDS

There are three choices of construction for halyards. They can either be all-wire, all-rope, or wire with rope tails. All-wire halyards are normally used for main or mizzen halyards on boats of about 12m (40ft) and above, but they are found occasionally on smaller boats. They are set up on reel winches which retain the fall entirely on an enclosed drum – just like a reel on a fishing rod. A brake is tightened to stop the halyard unwinding when it has been set up, and is released (or slackened off) to let the halyard run out when handling sail. *Very great care must be taken with reel winches not to trap your fingers.* When the halyard is run out as the sail is lowered, the turns on the drum slack off and tend to get entwined; they can also ride over each other when the halyard is set up. In either case the turns must be cleared, and it is then that fingers are most likely to be trapped and injured. The slack turns must be tightened (a slow business sometimes) before the winch can be used, and the turns that over-ride as the halyard is set up must be sorted out, otherwise unfair strains are put on the wire.

The reel winch must be quite large in order to get a big enough barrel diameter not to cripple the wire as it is wound on, and to accommodate all of the fall. The masthead sheaves too must be of large diameter to avoid crippling the wire, and a ratio of 12:1 for the diameter of the sheave to the diameter of the wire is suggested as a minimum.

While the all-wire halyard on its self-containing reel winch eliminates coils of rope hanging at the foot of the mast, and offers good, constant luff tension, it will swing about viciously when slack with the sail lowered. This allows the possibility of damage to both gear and crew besides the likelihood of its getting fouled up on something aloft. The wire must also be carefully guarded against crippling at all times as it will quickly destroy the strands.

At the opposite end to wire halyards are all-rope ones. Though unusual on racing boats because they cannot retain such high luff tension as wire halyards, all-rope ones are popular with cruising men because of their pleasantness to handle, their simplicity of splicing, and their longevity; price is also a consideration.

The introduction in recent years of synthetic fibre lines made of a braided core and plaited sheath has ousted three strand, hawser laid rope from its pre-eminent position for sheets and halyards. Now it is almost more common to see the core and sheath lines than the three strand type for running rigging. However, provided that a fairly soft three strand rope is chosen, there is nothing at all wrong with it for halyards. It should be soft for comfortable handling, and of a

pre-stretched type to reduce sagging under load.

While rope halyards have the advantage over wire of being usable with normal open barrel winches, it does mean that the falls have to be coiled and secured. I think this is a small price to pay though for the greater safety of a non-reel winch for, while it is certainly still possible to trap your fingers in the turns on these winches, it is far less likely to happen.

Chafe is the bane of all types of running rigging and careful precautions must be taken to minimise it. A wire halyard may happily saw its way through the wood or alloy surrounding a masthead sheave box if allowed to, probably without serious damage to its own structure, while a rope on the other hand will suffer chafe itself at that point. To this end it is well worth fitting over-sized sheaves, for although a sheave diameter to rope diameter ratio of only 5:1 is required for rope halyards (as opposed to the 12:1 minimum for wire) a larger sheave will carry the halyard clear of the sheave box and so reduce the chances of chafe. With mainsails this also helps to stop the top luff slide jamming in the track, because the halyard leads more fairly to the headboard.

In between the two extremes of all-wire and all-rope halyards comes the 'compromise halyard' constructed of wire with a rope tail. The idea is that the wire will allow greater luff tension and the rope will provide comfortable handling and make the use of open barrel winches possible. This last point is achieved by careful choice of lengths so that the wire winds onto the winch barrel leaving the rope tail to be made up on a cleat.

Both masthead sheaves and exit sheaves at the foot of the mast must be of large diameter to avoid crippling the wire, and the winch must also be of a larger drum diameter than would be needed for an all rope halyard. Unfortunately this of course puts up the price of the winch, but by moving up in size you also usually gain in power, which with a family crew may not be a bad thing. An underwinched boat can be hard work for a small or weak crew.

Problems can be encountered with the rope to wire splice because it forms a stiff section that will not readily pass round sheaves or winch drums. It is a mistake to try to ease this problem by cutting down on the number of tucks (and hence the length) of the splice. This will only weaken it.

Although, as I have said, many long term cruising people choose all-rope halyards, the most popular type on stock production boats of less than about 12m (40ft) is the part-wire, part-rope halyard. Above that size main halyards tend to be all-wire, but this is by no means always so and many still use the rope/wire

combination. Whether or not rope/wire halyards are either necessary or desirable on a family cruiser is a matter for some debate, but it is likely that any new boat over about 7m (23ft) will have them. It is up to you to decide whether or not you like them and whether or not to change them to all-rope when they need renewing.

## Internal or external halyards?

Most stock boats have internal halyards as they create less windage than external ones, and because a wire halyard passed through a plastic tube inside the mast has no chance to slap and chafe against it. If the wire were run either externally or internally but not through a tube, it would wear and chafe. This has to be watched with the part outside the mast when the sail is lowered as the wire can quickly cause a lot of damage both to itself and, for example, a spreader if it is allowed to saw back and forth against it while the boat rolls.

In my opinion the biggest argument against the use of internal halyards is that you cannot see what is happening to the part inside the mast. You have no idea if it is chafing, if a strand has parted, and if (as sometimes is the case) the rope to wire splice remains inside the mast, you cannot inspect it. In fact you can attach a light messenger and pull the halyard right through the mast to inspect its whole length, but few people take the trouble to do that.

Then there is the problem of renewing an internal halyard. If the old one is replaced before it parts, the new one can be attached to one end and hauled through, but if the old halyard parts, you are faced with the problem of passing a messenger down the mast to reeve off a new one. With an external halyard you should have noticed any chafe as it happened, but even if you did not and the halyard has parted, there is nothing like the same difficulty in reeving off a replacement. All that has to be done is to pass the rope through the masthead block or sheaves and take the ends down to the deck.

With external halyards there is a windage consideration and, particularly in heavy weather, this can be surprisingly high, but for the most part I think it is an acceptable penalty when the advantages are considered. I should make it clear at this point that I think wire halyards are better placed inside the mast because of the damage they are likely to do when flailing about if rigged externally. I would therefore only advocate the use of external halyards if you are prepared to accept all-rope construction.

At the beginning of this section I said that most stock boats are rigged with internal rope to wire halyards, but a rapidly increasing number of people are building boats from kits, bare hulls or plans, and these people have the opportunity of fitting out and arranging their boats exactly as they please. There is no reason at all why they should not order a mast with external rope halyards if they so choose.

## The right size for the job

It is hard to give accurate advice about the right size of wire or rope for halyards, since ease of handling almost takes precedence over strength, the simple reason being that all but the smallest diameter ropes will be sufficiently strong. The table below sets out some suggested sizes of polyester Braidline (a core-and-sheath rope) or pre-stretched polyester three strand.

| Boat LOA | | Main halyard diameter | | Jib halyard diameter | | Spinnaker halyard diameter | |
|---|---|---|---|---|---|---|---|
| (m) | (ft) | (mm) | (in) | (mm) | (in) | (mm) | (in) |
| 5 | 16 | 6 | 1/4 | 6 | 1/4 | 6 | 1/4 |
| 7 | 23 | 8 | 5/16 | 8 | 5/16 | 8 | 5/16 |
| 10 | 33 | 10 | 13/32 | 10 | 13/32 | 8 | 5/16 |
| 12 | 40 | 12 | 1/2 | 12 | 1/2 | 10 | 13/32 |
| 15 | 50 | 12 | 1/2 | 12 | 1/2 | 12 | 1/2 |

For stainless steel wire/rope halyards or all-wire ones the following is a rough guide.

| Boat LOA | | Main halyard wire diameter | | Jib halyard wire diameter | |
|---|---|---|---|---|---|
| (m) | (ft) | (mm) | (in) | (mm) | (in) |
| 5 | 16 | 4 | 5/32 | 4 | 5/32 |
| 7 | 23 | 5 | 13/64 | 5 | 13/64 |
| 10 | 33 | 6 | 1/4 | 6 | 1/4 |
| 12 | 40 | 8 | 5/16 | 8 | 5/16 |
| 15 | 50 | 8 | 5/16 | 8 | 5/16 |

## Spare halyards

There must obviously be one halyard for each sail normally set, but it is only prudent to provide at least one spare masthead halyard in case one of the others parts and cannot be replaced immediately. A masthead topping lift can double as a spare halyard if positioned and rigged with this possibility in mind, even if what is normally the fall has to be secured with a bowline to the head of a jib. Mind you, this can be improved upon if the topping lift has a thimble spliced into each end.

If twin headsails are used for running down wind two halyards will have to be provided. Racing crews may like to have a second spinnaker halyard available for spinnaker peeling. When a mizzen staysail is carried on a ketch or yawl there will have to be a separate halyard available for it. Perhaps the simplest boats in terms of number of halyards are cat boats or ones rigged with a single Chinese lugsail; they only carry one

halyard. Their problems start if that halyard parts.

## Fastening halyards to sails

Any method of fastening halyards to the heads of sails must be quick, simple and secure. Speed of operation makes both for efficiency in rapid sail changing and safety, by requiring as little time as possible to be spent on the foredeck. To this end they must obviously be simple to use; cold and wet reduce the gripping ability of fingers and so make any fiddly operations almost impossible. Lastly, any fastening must be secure against undoing by strain and flogging, the second being the more difficult to combine with the other requirements.

Headsails are changed far more frequently than mainsails or mizzens, and consequently main and mizzen halyards are normally fastened with shackles. These offer nearly total security with the use of shackle spanners or marlinspikes to tighten them, but the threads of their pins have to be kept greased for easy operation. The drawback to ordinary shackles is that the pins can easily be dropped overboard, and for this reason they are not recommended. The form that is recommended is the captive pin shackle. With this type the pin does not have a thread but is shaped like a key;

the protruding key passes through a slot in one side of the shackle and is turned to prevent its going back again, while on the other side the pin is in a circular hole that will not allow the key to drop out when the shackle is open; thus the pin is captive and cannot be lost. When choosing this type of shackle, try to pick out ones whose pins fit properly but not too tightly, and which have large enough heads for cold fingers to grip and turn.

A lot of people use these same captive pin shackles for attaching headsail halyards, while others go for the piston type snap shackle. Both forms of fastening are quite secure, though in my experience the snap shackle has slightly superior resistance to opening when flogging about. On the other hand I have known snap shackles to be tripped when short cords attached to the pistons have been fouled on rigging. It must be a matter of personal preference which you choose, but I think the snap shackle is a little faster to use and a little easier with cold hands, provided that a short lanyard is attached to the piston. Like ordinary shackles, snap shackles must be kept greased for smooth operation.

A word of warning about both of these systems for attaching halyards. As the boat pitches and rolls, particularly with wire halyards and/or wire strops on the heads of the sails, the shackles will swing about wildly and can cause serious injury. They are likely also to wrap themselves round the forestay if just the right amount of tension is not kept on them, but this is less important than the possibility of an eye or head injury. Beware.

## Halyard winches

Good winches are not cheap and it therefore makes sense not to use ones that are either bigger or more complicated than necessary. Boats up to about 8m (26ft) do not really need halyard winches at all as there is no problem for most people in swigging the halyards up hard and, even if some difficulty is experienced, it is simple to incorporate a two part purchase in the halyard fall or to use a tack tackle. Above this size a halyard winch does make sense, but it need only be a fairly small single speed winch. Only large boats need to go up to two speed winches for normal halyard use.

If an all-wire main halyard is used then it must have a reel winch to take the fall, but other halyards are best served by open barrel winches with the falls cleated and coiled. Whether top or bottom action winches are chosen will depend on positioning, personal preference and cost. Top action winches, ones with the handle inserted at the free end of the barrel, must have their handles removed and stowed safely but close at hand. Bottom action winches usually have their handles permanently located at the base end of the barrel so there is no chance of losing them. The fact that the handle cannot be removed means that it often fouls the halyard and other lines but, unlike a top action handle, it does not obstruct you when you are trying to put an extra turn round the barrel. The fixed handle will swing round some way when the halyard is slipped round the drum and then stop; the top action handle *must never* be left in place, as it swings right round and can cause nasty injuries.

When choosing a winch for a halyard of the rope/wire type, the barrel diameter must be large enough not to cripple the wire.

## Tack tackles and downhauls

On smaller boats there is no reason why the weight of the sail and boom (in the case of mainsails and mizzens) should not be made to work for you when setting up the luff, by the use of a tack tackle or gooseneck downhaul. The halyard is set up either by swigging or by using a two part purchase in the halyard or small winch, and the weight of the sail is then turned to your advantage by hauling down at the tack. For a headsail, the tack tackle can either be fitted between the stemhead fitting and the tack, or a line from the tack can be brought aft through a block at the stemhead to a tackle on deck. With a mainsail or mizzen the tackle is simply run between the gooseneck and the deck or mast step. This does of course presume a sliding gooseneck on a short length of track.

## Siting halyard winches and cleats

The question here is whether to fit the halyard winches and cleats on the mast near its foot (at or below boom level) or to place them somewhere on deck. The more usual practice on stock family boats is to place them all on the mast; main halyard one side, headsail the other and perhaps spinnaker on either side. Doing this concentrates a lot of stress in one area of the mast which, though it may not weaken the spar significantly, certainly does not strengthen it. From a working point of view too it is not ideal to have the winches and cleats on the mast. With them there the crew must either stand up to get leverage on the winch handle, or kneel down and not be able to set up the luff as hard as he might want. Reefing operations involving one person on the halyard and another winding a roller reefing handle can also get complicated if both people have to be at the mast.

On the whole I think it is better to take

the winches and cleats off the mast and put them on deck, either close by the foot of the mast or right aft at the cockpit end of the coachroof. This latter arrangement means that the halyards can be handled from the safer working area of the cockpit, but it can only really be used where there is no step in the coachroof, otherwise the halyards will have to be led through bullseyes at the change of level.

If the halyards are internal they can be led out of the mast through sheaves at deck level, thus avoiding the S-bend they would have to go through to be led to mast-mounted winches from exits higher up. Placing the winches on deck means more room around them, but it does also make movement on deck more difficult, and this is another argument in favour of leading all the halyards aft to the cockpit, especially if they are led under removable covers on which you can stand. I say 'removable covers' rather than just 'under the deck', because it would be a hard job to thread new halyards through conduit piping along the length of the coachroof but, if you can just lift hatches and pass the lines through a couple of fairleads, there's no problem.

Having the halyards back at the cockpit allows someone there to ease them away as another crew member either reefs the sail or hands it. This is perhaps exemplified on Chinese lugsail rigged boats, where all the sail controls are led to a single position for easy operation by one person, whether the sail is to be set, handed, reefed or trimmed.

Again, by leading all the halyards aft, it is possible to save on winches by making one serve several purposes. This technique has been developed on racing yachts and is sensible in terms of saving on cost and weight. The idea is to bring all the halyards aft to a row of stoppers placed ahead of a single (powerful) winch. A halyard is set up using the winch, the stopper is applied to jam the line, and it is them removed from the winch and held under tension by the stopper (which is like a manually operated jam cleat). With that line removed from the winch any other halyard can be put on and set up.

Some people have managed to take slab reefing lines back to the same battery of stoppers, thus making it possible to reef the mainsail without leaving the cockpit. An excellent safety plan. Incidentally, these jammers are the only cleats which should be placed on the same side of a winch as the load. Otherwise a cleat should always be on the opposite side, with the winch between it and the load.

The final and rather morbid argument for keeping winches and cleats off the mast is that, should you lose the mast, you still have the winches, and they may help when setting up a jury rig.

## Pinrails

A few boats use a pinrail at the foot of the mast or across the shrouds or along the toerail. Admittedly this is something normally associated with gaff rig, where it is important to keep halyards clear of the mast so that they do not jam in the gaff jaws, but it also has other advantages. The biggest of these is perhaps that the pins can be longer than the horns of normal mast-mounted cleats. Modern synthetic lines require a good number of turns round a cleat to hold securely, and all too many mast-mounted cleats (and others for that matter) have horns that are so short that it is next to impossible to get the necessary turns to stay on. The pins can be of a good length without interfering with other lines, which is usually the limiting factor on mast-mounted cleats. A pinrail can also carry more lines; for instance you may have mast-mounted cleats for main halyard, headsail, spinnaker, burgee and topping lift, and then have little room left for spinnaker pole topping lift and downhaul (let alone the gear for twin headsails), spare halyards and anything else required. A couple of pinrails can cope with this lot easily and, as an adjunct to normal cleats, they are invaluable.

## Tidying up the falls

With mast-mounted winches, halyard falls are usually coiled and hung from the cleat or tucked between the standing part and the mast. With winches set on deck, the coiled fall can be held under a length of shock cord to stop it spreading all over the deck. This system can also be used instead of hanging the coils from cleats on the mast, where they are liable to foul the clew of the headsail when tacking. Another way of keeping things tidy is an open box for the falls at the foot of the mast, where they are flaked down ready to run out as the halyard is cast off.

Halyards led aft to the cockpit can be stowed in canvas pouches on the cockpit face of the cabin bulkhead. Here they are out of the way and are most unlikely to be washed overboard.

An intriguing system I have heard described is to have an endless halyard, that is to say one with both ends fast to the head of the sail, so that a downhaul is automatically provided, and the bight of the halyard is made up on the cleat, leaving no loose ends.

Whatever system you choose for halyard falls, it is important that the line be easily laid out to run free if the sail has to be lowered quickly. To this end the falls must be made up tidily as soon as the sail is set, and stowed so that they do not become tangled and need re-coiling.

Always remember to put a figure of eight stopper knot in the end of the halyard so that, should it be allowed to fly free, it cannot run through the mast sheaves and is therefore retrievable without the trouble of reeving off a new halyard. A good practice for external halyards is to attach their bitter ends to swivel eyes at the foot of the mast so they cannot run aloft and be lost, nor can they get twisted.

### Winch handle stowage

Some sort of secure stowage close to the mast winches is required, unless you choose to keep the handles somewhere aft in a locker and bring them forward each time a sail change is made. A lot of boats are fitted with plastic pockets in which the winch handles are stowed, but two cheaper (though less sightly) answers are pieces of shock cord or lengths of plastic hose pipe. Either will hold the handle adequately, but I admit they don't look so smart.

Don't try attaching the handles to the mast with lines, these will certainly foul up in use. Neither would I be happy with the use of loops round the wrists while winching, as you would then be unable to let go of the handle instantly should you need to.

Larger craft can make good use of a locker at the mast, either sunk into the deck or mounted on it. This can hold winch handles, sail tiers and, if large enough, sail covers and bags.

### Stop that noise

Halyards tapping against metal masts make an infuriating din when you are trying to sleep, and are anti-social in port. There is no excuse for leaving slapping halyards as they can so easily be tied away from the mast (either with light line or shockcord) when snugging everything down on deck. Better still is to take them all off the mast and secure them forward on the pulpit or out to the rails, but do allow for the possibility of having to put to sea quickly–don't lash them so much that it takes you half an hour to undo.

Even if for some unbelievable reason you don't mind the sound of rattling halyards, think of how they are chafing– not to say annoying the boat next door.

### Sail watching

When hoisting a sail it is important to watch it go up and set clear. To help this, if you are right handed, have the fore halyard on a winch on the starboard side of the mast so that, as you winch (with your right hand), you are facing forward,

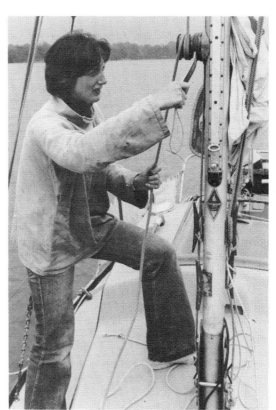

looking at the headsail. Place the main halyard to port so that, as you work its winch, you will again be facing the sail as it is hoisted. This is the reverse of the traditional mainsail-to-starboard, jib-to-port custom, but at least has some reasoning behind it.

PHOTO 1
In these pictures the deckhand is working at the mast in a secure stance with both legs braced against possible movement of the boat. On the left, the man is watching the mainsail as he hoists to see that nothing snags aloft, while the woman on the right is fitting the winch handle prior to setting up the genoa luff. In each situation the halyard is sited to allow easy handling while watching the sails go up.

CHAPTER FOUR

# RUNNING RIGGING

SHEETS

## Chafe

The most insidious and one of the more dangerous forms of damage on a boat is chafe. All the time she is afloat, whether at sea or lying to a mooring, a boat is moving and, as she moves, something rubs back and forth against something else; one of them wears away. It often goes unnoticed until a piece of gear fails, causing annoyance if not serious trouble.

This may sound a trifle dramatic, but it is true, chafe must be guarded against in every way possible and nothing can be over-protected against it. Running rigging is obviously susceptible to chafe and hence its mention here.

As sheets are surged round a winch they will naturally begin to wear, that has to be accepted, and with some ropes the beginnings of wear roughen the surface actually improving its grip on the drum but, if a sheet is allowed to rub and saw across a guardrail for any length of time, it will chafe through. By 'any length of time' I mean as little as a few hours – a couple of watches during the night, when chafing may continue unobserved. Therefore, this must be dealt with as soon as it begins, either by changing the lead of the sheet or by binding the rubbing area with canvas or rags.

When the boom is squared off the mainsheet usually lies across the upper guardwire, where it will begin to chafe as the boat rolls her way downwind. Even with a foreguy rigged on the boom there will be a little lift and the sheet will rub. A lot of people accept this unquestioningly, but designers and builders (particulary home boatbuilders) can often avoid the problem by using a different mainsheet system. The most obvious is to raise the horse from deck level to the level of the upper guardwire. This can be done quite simply by incorporating a bar which will act as the horse in the construction of the pushpit. The lower mainsheet block slides along this bar at the same height as the top of the pushpit and the sheet cannot then chafe on the guardrails.

Admittedly this can only be done on boats whose booms extend well aft, those with short booms and cockpits going right aft to the transom have a more difficult problem as the mainsheet usually falls naturally to a point well forward in the cockpit. In this case it may be necessary to accept that the sheet will lie across the guardrails, and put plastic tubing over the wires to act as a roller. It must be loose enough to turn easily with the movement of the mainsheet, but one thing to watch is that the roller makes the upper wire an insecure handhold, and this disadvantage needs to be weighed against the advantage of reduced chafe. The answer may be to have a length of tube that can be slipped onto the wire when the mainsheet is run off and

removed at other times. This can be done by cutting the tube spirally and winding it onto the wire in exactly the same way as is done on the shrouds to stop sheets chafing against them.

In times past shroud rollers were made of split bamboo taped round the shrouds, but they are now made of plastic piping which is either slipped onto the rigging wire before the eyesplice is put into the end (or the terminal is fitted), or else it is split spirally and wound on afterwards. The former method means that it is permanently in place, but there is no chance of the sheets pressing themselves into the spiral splits, while the split tubing allows this possibility if it is put on with the spiral the wrong way, but it does offer ease of renewal should it wear out before the rigging needs replacing. (The spiral should be left handed on the starboard shrouds and right handed to port). In either case, they should be fitted loosely and, if possible, have a plastic ball fitted at the lower end to prevent them slipping down onto the splice or terminal and jamming so that they can't revolve.

It's not only guardrails and shrouds that sheets can chafe against. Care must be taken to tape all split pins and ends of wire used to secure turnbuckles; alternatively a length of clear plastic pipe can be slipped over them – clear so that you can see what's going on without having to remove them for inspection. Cleats must have smooth edges; some are designed with rather hard corners and these should be avoided. You must keep a sharp lookout for chafe points and deal with them straight away.

## Choosing sheets

As I said when talking about halyards, it is hard to give specific advice about the size of rope to use for sheets since it is comfort and ease of handling that is so important. Strength obviously cannot be ignored, but it is quite common to use a 10 mm (13/32 in) line for the sheets of both a dinghy and a 9 m (30-footer). Clearly if the line is strong enough for the large boat, it is more than adequate for the dinghy and must have been chosen on other grounds, usually ease of handling. There is a physical limit to how small a line you can grip and haul on with any power and, considering the possibility of having to work in cold, wet conditions, I would suggest that this lower limit is about 10 mm (13/32 in). The table below gives a guide to rope sizes based on the core-and-sheath polyester Braidline rope which is excellent for sheets, being strong, supple, soft to grip and long lasting. Three strand hawser laid rope can be used, but it is generally harder on the hands.

| Boat LOA | | Main or jib sheet diameter | | Genoa sheet diameter | | Spinnaker Sheet/guy diameter | |
|---|---|---|---|---|---|---|---|
| (m) | (ft) | (mm) | (in) | (mm) | (in) | (mm) | (in) |
| 5 | 16 | 10 | 13/32 | 10 | 13/32 | 8 | 9/16 |
| 7 | 23 | 10 | 13/32 | 10 | 13/32 | 10 | 13/32 |
| 10 | 33 | 10 | 13/32 | 12 | 1/2 | 12 | 1/2 |
| 12 | 40 | 12 | 1/2 | 14 | 9/16 | 14 | 9/16 |
| 15 | 50 | 12 | 1/2 | 16 | 5/8 | 16 | 5/8 |

There are many unbranded, cheap plaited and laid ropes on the market, but most of them are of inferior quality to the ones from well-known manufacturers and may break down quickly under the influence of ultra violet rays from sunlight if they have not been treated with an inhibitor. It is rarely worth taking the risk of broken gear by using these cheap lines. The best material for sheets is polyester (sold under such trade names as Terylene, Dacron, Tergal), as it stretches far less than nylon which would need constant trimming, and is more resistant to abrasion than some of the other man made fibre ropes.

## Attaching sheets

Mainsheets are attached pretty well permanently to the boom by way of a multi-part upper block, or a number of single blocks shackled onto either a swivelling end fitting or a fixed metal strap or claw. The swivel is necessary if roller reefing gear is fitted, unless a metal claw is used that lets the boom revolve within its arms. These claws are not ideal, as they can chafe the reefed sail despite having nylon rollers on the ends of the arms. The fixed metal strap can be used with a slab or points reefing system where it is desired to attach the mainsheet at some distance from the end of the boom.

Occasionally the mainsheet is attached at one point and then led along the boom by way of a series of blocks to a control position elsewhere, for instance to a place where either the helmsman or a sheet hand can trim it. This happens more often on racing craft than family cruisers, where the simplest effective system is usually provided.

The lower end of the mainsheet is normally controlled by a slide on a horse to give lateral adjustment when it is required to hold the boom down as well as just 'in' or 'out'. It is usual these days to have a single mainsheet fall, but some boats are rigged with a double ended sheet which lets adjustment be made from either side of the cockpit. However, if the fall is led to a cleat amidships this is unnecessary, as it can be reached equally well from either side.

Boats rigged with one or more Chinese lugsails have a more complicated sheeting system, with many parts led from spans between the ends of the full length sail battens. Like a normal mainsheet however, these are permanently rigged and culminate in a single hauling part led from a fixed point, often on the top rail of the pushpit. They are no more complicated to use than conventional mainsheets, but would take longer to rig if needing replacement.

Headsail sheets are attached to their sails in a variety of ways, depending on whether they are a single line seized together at the middle to form an eye which is attached to the clew, or else two separate lines, each attached independently to the clew. If they consist of two separate lines they will usually be fastened to the clew with bowlines or variations on bowlines. This is a quick and easy knot both to tie and untie, and there is no need for anything more complicated. Some people prefer to finish the bowline with the bitter end on the outside of the loop rather than on the inside. If you are skipper you can choose; if you are in the crew you do as you are told and argue the merits of one against the other later, preferably ashore. Whatever the case, the crewman *must* learn this knot, which is the nearest thing to the all-purpose knot afloat.

Where the sheet is a single line with an eye seized in the middle, it is common to find it attached to the clew with a piston action snap shackle which is quick to use, but which can cause a nasty injury if it catches you on the head while flogging about. Occasionally people use a shackle with either a captive pin or a screw pin. The former is comparable with the snap shackle in ease of use, but is again likely to cause injury, as indeed is the screw pin shackle which has the added drawback of an easily lost pin. Don't use these, they are fiddly, slow, dangerous when the sail is flogging and much too easy to lose.

The best method in my opinion for attaching a single line sheet is to form a soft eye in the middle which will pass through the clew ring (probably a larger one than is normally fitted) and can then be held in position by passing a short, doubled length of stiff rope through it. This stiff piece of rope can either be seized to one of the sheets so that it isn't lost when the sheets are not in use, or it can be passed through the eye and then have its two parts seized together, thus making it captive but free to move about on the seized sheet eye. Once the eye in the sheets has been passed through the clew ring and the stiff rope has been passed through the eye, the tension in the sheets settles the whole lot firmly in place and it won't come undone when the sail flogs, nor will it cause serious injury if it clips you round the ear. A similar alternative to this is a strop with a button knot at one end. The loop is passed through the clew ring and the eye in the sheets, then the button knot is passed through the loop. Tension on the sheets holds it secure, but it can come undone when flogging hard.

## Headsail sheet leads

Whereas it used to be sufficient to say that a headsail sheet should make a narrow angle downwards from the mitre line, nowadays sailmakers are using so many different sail constructions, some having no mitre and others more than one, that it is no longer possible to give such simple advice. On a modern yacht it is common to find at least one track on deck each side, to take sheet lead blocks and to give the facility of fore and aft adjustment in order to alter the tension in the foot and leech of the sail. If you can determine exact lead positions for each sail under average conditions, then there is no reason why you should not use the older fixed position bullseyes but, by doing so, you do eliminate the possibility of adjustment. If you can accept that, fine, otherwise you will need some sort of sheet lead track.

Sheet lead tracks are usually made of an alloy extrusion shaped in cross section like a T, with a block attached to a sliding car that fits on the top bar of the T. The car can be fixed at any point along the track either by tightening down a clamping screw, or dropping a spring loaded pin into one of a series of holes in the track. The screw allows an infinite variety of positions, while the drop pin can only be used where there is a hole; but there are a lot of these so the choice of position is wide. Some boats carry the lead blocks on an alloy toerail, either as a car sliding in the same way as on the T track, or as a snatch block clipped into any one of a series of holes.

Sophisticated racing boats may have several tracks on each sidedeck, to allow choice of athwartships sheeting angle to the centreline, as well as fore and aft positioning. Whether or not you really need to fit more than one track is best decided after consultation with your sailmaker.

## Marking sheet lead positions

We will say more in detail about sheeting angles in the next chapter but, for the time being, it needs to be said that there is no point in having variable position sheet leads if you are not going to make at least some use of them. In other words, why have a length of expensive track if you never move the lead blocks when changing sails? The point is that each sail needs to be sheeted at the correct angle to give the right leech and foot tensions, and having a block on a track makes

adjustment possible. Each sail is cut differently and, because of this, when changing from one sail to another it is necessary to move the lead blocks to new positions. To facilitate this it is worth marking on each track the right position for the lead block for each headsail. For example a figure 1 painted on the deck by the position for the lead block when the No 1 genoa is in use, a 2 by the place for it when the No 2 is set, and so on. Alternatively a letter G for the genoa position, a W for the working jib and an S for the storm or spitfire jib. These positions should be marked when the sail is setting correctly to a wind in about the middle of that sail's wind strength range. For example, if you use a genoa up to the lower end of Force 4, say 12 knots of wind, then mark its sheet lead position in a Force 2, or about 6 knots of wind. The working jib and storm jib require more wind than this for adjustment and marking, but there is no need to go looking for a gale just to set up the storm jib lead blocks.

By doing this for each sail, the lead blocks can quickly be positioned when changing headsails with the certainty that they are nearly in the right place, and that the sail won't be sheeted in with a taut foot and a bellying leech (or vice versa). If you are really keen, you may want to make adjustments after the sail is set and drawing according to the prevailing wind and sea conditions, but for most sailing the set will be OK like this.

## Siting winches and cleats

Some requirements for good siting of winches and their associated cleats were discussed in Chapter 1, and they may be summarized thus:

a. It is essential to have a fair lead into the winch for the sheet.

b. There must be adequate space at the winch for grinding in and tailing (either by the winch hand or a second crewman).

c. The cleat must be on the opposite side of the winch to the incoming sheet, and must be readily accessible for turning up the tail and casting it off.

d. The surface round the winch should be non-slip.

e. The winch handle must not foul the guardrails or dodgers.

The average family boat of medium size will have a headsail sheet winch on each cockpit coaming, usually on a pedestal moulded as an extension of the coaming, and perhaps a spinnaker sheet/ guy winch abaft that on the coaming itself. This arrangement is adequate if the requirements listed above are met. Unfortunately it is common to find that, although a winch is slightly angled, it is not sufficient to keep the turns lying correctly on the barrel. This seems to be the commonest error when installing winches apart from putting the cleats on the same side as the load.

The 'two winches each side' arrangement works perfectly well in practice but, if you are starting from scratch (say when building from a bare hull), you might consider other set-ups. One that I think has attractions is a centrally mounted winch, either on the bridgedeck or a special pedestal, to which are led the headsail sheets by way of fairleads in the cockpit coamings. The advantages are that you only have to buy one winch, thus saving money, and that you may very well be able to achieve a better working position than is possible with the winches mounted on the coamings. The spinnaker sheet and guy will still need their separate winches.

Larger racing boats have far more winches than a family cruiser and these tend to be grouped in 'farms' at strategic points on the deck. Many offshore racers have what are called coffee grinder winches. These are pedestals, with handles like bicycle pedals (only operated by hand) which are mechanically linked to work remote winch drums. The idea is that more power can be applied to these multi-geared winches. As for any other winch though, coffee grinders must be sited on a secure working platform.

## Cleats

The basic requirements for a cleat are that the line should lead fair to it, that it should hold the line turned up on it securely, that the line can be cast off readily even when under load, and that the cleat should not cripple or otherwise damage the line belayed on it.

The choice lies between the conventional cleat with its double horns, and any one of a number of different types of jamming cleat. The horned cleat should be angled at 10-20 degrees open to the incoming lead, and the line to be made up on it should be led into the back of the cleat, a full round turn taken, and then a series of figures of eight put round the horns. Not having the cleat angled, or leading into the front of the cleat, may jam the line and prevent its being cast off quickly. Many of these cleats have rather short horns, insufficient to stop the turns of a springy synthetic line jumping off. In this case it is best to fit a cleat with longer horns but, failing this, a jamming turn can be put on. This turn *must* be slipped if it is used, otherwise there will come the time when it really does jam. It should not normally be necessary to use a jamming turn, and it is not good practice.

The two main types of jamming cleat are the double cam type, where the rope is held between two spring-loaded toothed cams, and the grooved vee type, where the rope is pushed down into a vee with a set of notches that grip the rope; in both cases the grip increases with load. These jamming cleats both work better on a laid rope than a plaited one, and both suffer the drawback that the line must be hardened in slightly before it can be released – which contravenes one of the prime requirements of a cleat, that the line can be released even under full load. Nevertheless, jam cleats are widely used and do have acceptable applications. I'm not sure though that they are a good thing for making sheets fast. Unlike horn cleats, jamming cleats must be exactly in line with the incoming rope.

One other type of cleat is common, and that is a variation on the double horn type where one horn is short and the other is cut with a vee under it. A turn is taken round the cleat, and the load on the line settles it into the vee, thus jamming it. Figure of eight turns make all secure. With this type, the line does not have to be hardened in to release it but, if you are not positive in your releasing actions, the line re-jams itself before it has been thrown completely clear. The shorter stub end must be away from the load, with the jamming vee towards the pull; the whole cleat should be angled so that the vee does not quite close the circle with the angle of the incoming line.

## Self-tailing winches

On a small to medium size boat it is quite easy to grind in on a winch and tail the sheet at the same time; that is to say you heave the handle round with one hand, while hauling on the tail of the sheet with the other, to stop it slipping on the drum and to give a little help in getting it in hard. With a larger boat and larger sails it is normal for one person to grind using both hands and all his strength, while a second person tails and eventually belays. A modern development is the self-tailing winch, which makes it possible for a single operator to grind in using both hands on the winch handle, while the winch itself does the tailing. Clearly this makes for more efficient working, as the best of both worlds is achieved – one man only is needed and he can exert his full force in turning the handle.

The self-tailing winch is exactly the same as a conventional one up to the top of the barrel, but then it changes. A disc is mounted on top of the barrel with a vee cut round its circumference. Inside the vee there are grooves exactly like those on a vee-type jam cleat. The sheet is wound on the barrel in normal fashion and is then led past a stripper (guide) and into this grooved channel. As the winch barrel is turned, the tail is pulled off by the stripper and kept under constant tension by the revolving jam cleat. To cast the sheet off, it is pulled out of the groove and the turns unwound from the barrel. The sheet cannot simply be pulled vertically, as it can with a conventional winch, since it will foul on the stripper. Consequently tacking may be a little slower until you become accustomed to the winches, and care must be taken not to put kinks in the sheet or to trap your fingers in the turns. Hold the *heel* of the hand against the turns when pulling the sheet out of the cleat to stop them slipping before you're ready.

As the tail of the sheet is held in what is effectively a jam cleat there is no need to cleat it elsewhere. Cleats should still be provided though, in case of any problems and should you need the winch for another task.

## Mainsheet tracks

The old name of mainsheet horse seems to have disappeared just as finally as the old iron bar and traveller to which the name applies. The advent of alloy extrusions in either T or X form with nylon wheeled travellers to carry the lower mainsheet blocks changed the whole nature of mainsail control. Suddenly people became aware that not only did the amount of twist and the sheeting angle of the headsail matter, but so too did these points on the mainsail. Of course I do not doubt that many people were aware of this earlier, but at the family cruiser end of the spectrum we were content to sheet the mainsail to a horse with a traveller that flew from one end to the other when we tacked. Now the art is much more refined and, even at its most basic, we move the traveller some way towards the centreline going to windward and out to the end of the track going down wind.

Not all boats have mainsheet tracks, but as so many newcomers to cruising boats have been used to the fine adjustments possible on all parts of a racing dinghy's rigging and sails, boat builders have had to cater for them to some extent by providing these tracks. The club racing fraternity also demands that such adjustments be made possible, so it is popular all round – and it does offer better sail control, which must be a good thing.

The question of where best to put the mainsheet track is very much in the hands of the designer. The modern short-boomed mainsail often means that the sheet has to come down to a track across the cockpit, thus effectively dividing it in two with the helmsman abaft the track and the sheet hands forward of it. If the boom is longer (or the mast further aft) the track may be on the after cockpit coaming. The options then include sheeting some distance inboard from the end of the boom to a track on the bridgedeck, or to

blocks on either side of the companionway (which can make getting in and out of the cabin difficult), or to a track just forward of the hatch. One of the best positions for a mainsheet track or horse however is still across the pushpit at a level with the top rail because, in this position, there is no chafe on the guardrails when the mainsheet is paid off.

We will examine the use of the mainsheet traveller and track in controlling sail shape in the next chapter.

## Preventing sheets fouling

When tacking it is common for slack headsail sheets to get foul of mast cleats or halyard coils, thus holding the sail aback and ruining the tack. This trouble can be reduced greatly or even avoided entirely, in one of three ways: have no cleats or halyards made up on the mast; fit a canvas coat round the mast which covers the cleats and coiled halyards; run a line from the mast above the cleats down to the deck some distance forward. Any of these works, but the last is usually the easiest to arrange, and if a heavy enough line is used has the added advantage of offering another good handhold on the foredeck. Some designs incorporate an inner forestay as part of the standing rigging and this serves the same purpose (in addition to its mast

supporting job). A roller tube on this stay
or on the improvised one will reduce its
security as a handhold, but might make
the sheets and sail slide round it more
readily. Which is better, a secure
handhold or the possibility of easier
tacking? The answer must vary from boat
to boat, but I would suggest the handhold
is normally of greater value.

# CHAPTER FIVE
# SAIL HANDLING

Time spent moving fore and aft with cumbersome sail bags, bending on and unhanking sails up in the pulpit, working at the mast with both hands, bagging sails, is all 'time at risk'. It is all too easy for a sail that is being unhanked to fill with wind and balloon up, possibly throwing anyone trying to muzzle it off balance; or the boat may take a sudden lurch while you are hauling on a halyard so that, with both hands occupied, you are in real danger of going overboard. Clearly we must try to keep the time spent at risk to a minimum, and that means developing efficient, time-saving techniques for sail changing and handling.

Perhaps the ultimate in safe, efficient sail handling is the Chinese lugsail rig where sails are set, trimmed, reefed and handed all from one position of safety in either the cockpit or companionway. The fully battened sails drop into lazyjacks (double topping lifts) and, because the battens and yards hold them down, you do not normally even have to go on deck to put on tiers. For bermudan rigged boats the equivalent must be a roller reefing headsail with mainsail reefing operated from the cockpit. For the majority of sailing people however it is necessary to make the trip forward, and so we need to have an organized pattern of working that will reduce the number of movements fore and aft to a minimum and will keep the time taken as low as possible. That does not mean rushing things, for haste is likely to make people careless, but it means such things as taking the halyard winch handle with you rather than having to make a separate trip aft to the cockpit to collect it.

## Bending sails on

A lot of people bend on their mainsail at the beginning of the season when the boat is commissioned and take it off at the end, using a sail cover to protect it when it is not in use. Others prefer to take the sail off the boom and bag it up at the end of each outing. In either case the mainsail is normally bent on or taken off when the boat is lying to her mooring or at anchor, which makes the job that much easier for, although the sail is awkward to handle, the working platform is fairly steady.

All the time a sail is out of its bag and not bent on it is likely to balloon up and cause trouble. Always, therefore, bag sails with the foot at the top of the bag and, in the case of headsails, with the tack at the mouth, or for mainsails, with the clew at the mouth of the bag. By doing this, the sail can be partly bent on (and so controlled) while the bulk of it is still in the bag. In the case of mainsails it is possible to start feeding the foot slides onto the boom track, or the foot bolt rope

into the boom groove, before all of the sail is taken out of the bag. Once the sail is out, the bag can either be left tied onto a cabintop grabrail until the sail is ready, or it must be stowed away before it is blown overboard.

While it is quite possible for one person to bend the mainsail onto the boom, two people make the job easier, as one can haul the foot out along the boom while the other feeds the rope into the groove or the slides into the track at the gooseneck. The mainsheet must be belayed so that the boom cannot swing about if it is held by a topping lift, and it must be left in the gallows or crutch if either of these is used. Always work from the windward side of the boom so that if the sail balloons up it does so away from you – this applies to any sail.

Once the foot has been fed onto the boom the tack must be secured, and this is usually done with either a shackle to an eye on the boom or a drop-nose pin fitting through cheeks on either side of the tack cringle. If you intend to take the main off frequently it is more convenient to use a well lubricated drop-nose pin if you can, but secure it with a cord to avoid loss.

After the tack has been secured the outhaul is attached to the clew and is tensioned. The outhaul can take any number of forms, but in the case of small boats it is usually a hand-tightened lashing to an eye on the boom, while larger boats may have a line led round a block and forward along the boom to a cleat near the gooseneck, from which point tension can be adjusted while underway. Still larger boats may incorporate a tackle or winch for tensioning the clew. How tight the foot should be is a matter for experiment, but generally it should be hauled out until there are stretch creases just appearing parallel to the boom before the sail is hoisted.

That's the foot dealt with and now, if it hasn't already happened, the rest of the sail is taken out of the bag and we can turn out attention to the luff. The first step is to straighten it out by running your hand from tack to head (not the other way round), taking out any twists as you go. On reaching the head, feed the top slide into the mast track at the gate, or feed the end of the luff rope into the mast groove. Go on feeding in and moving the slides up the mast until they are all in and the gate can be closed. Now the sail is captive on two edges and can only flog about, it cannot go over the side or get out of control. In the case of mainsails with luff ropes fitting into a mast groove, the sail must be tied down to the boom when the head has been put in the groove to stop it blowing about. Alternatively, if through-mast roller reefing is fitted, the sail can be rolled round the boom rather than stowed up on top of it.

Now the battens. These will either be tied into their pockets or will slip in at an angle and have to be pushed down behind the closed part of the pocket. It is wise to label the battens, either by numbering or by notation such as 'upper' 'middle', and 'lower'. This saves having to offer up each batten to see if it is the right one for that pocket. Work systematically from head to foot (or the other way round) to avoid missing one out and having to go back, thus wasting time.

If it is not planned to hoist the main immediately, it is as well now to put some tiers round it and the boom to stop it blowing about.

Before attaching the main halyard to the head of the sail check that it is free to run and is not twisted or fouled aloft. It can be secured to the head with either an ordinary shackle, one of the captive pin variety, or a snap shackle. I prefer not to use an ordinary shackle as there is the chance of losing it or its pin, and would rather see one of the other two fitted. After shackling the halyard on, take a bight of it under a mast cleat and bowse down on the fall and belay it. This holds the sail down and stops it blowing up the mast. Of course this can only be done if there are cleats on the mast or a pin rail at its foot, otherwise a long tier can be put round the sail and boom between the head and the mast so that it bears down on the slides themselves.

The boom vang or kicking strap must now be attached to the underside of the boom. This is a tackle that holds the boom down and stops it skying when squared off before the wind. It runs from an attachment point under the boom down to the heel of the mast, or to the after side of the mast at deck level if it is keel not deck stepped. The attachment to the boom is normally either a shackle of some sort to a metal strap or slider in a groove, or a key into a slot in the boom. Once both ends are secured, overhaul the line (ensure that it runs freely through the blocks) and leave it slack.

Finally the gooseneck downhaul must be attached, overhauled and left loose. This is a tackle for adjusting luff tension without touching the main halyard. Not all boats have them, those that do not are fitted with a fixed gooseneck and use the halyard to adjust luff tension. Whether it is necessary or not depends very largely on the cut of the sail and on class rules if racing.

The mainsail has now been bent on and prepared for hoisting, so we can now look at the headsail.

Whenever a headsail is bagged up it should be done so that the tack is at the top and can be pulled out first. By attaching the tack before taking the sail out of its bag you do not risk losing the sail overboard if it balloons up and gets out of control. It may go in the water, but at least it cannot be lost completely. First job then is to tie the bag to the guardrail near the pulpit and attach the tack so that the luff and hanks are uppermost. There are a variety of ways in which the tack can be secured. On some boats it is shackled directly to the stemhead fitting, on others it attaches to a tack pennant or span, and on others again it goes onto a tack tackle. If it goes directly to a stemhead fitting it is likely to be fastened with either a shackle or a snap shackle, though racing boats in recent years have been using a simple stainless steel hook welded onto the stemhead fitting which goes through the tack cringle. This is clearly quick to use, but there is no security until there is tension on the luff unless a shockcord retainer is rigged on the hook. With either a pennant or tackle the ubiquitous snap shackle is the likeliest method of fastening. If there is a tackle, overhaul it now before you have to search about under all the sail when it has been hanked on.

The idea of attaching directly to the stemhead fitting is to keep the headsail as close to the deck as possible (taken to its ultimate in the deck-sweeping genoas used when racing) to reduce the amount of air lost under the sail's foot. The drawbacks are that you lose forward vision and the foot chafes on the guardrails when the sail is freed off down wind. In my opinion a cruising boat should use a pennant or, if needed, a tackle which allows the tack to set at the same level as the upper bar of the pulpit. This may be slightly inefficient in terms of air lost under the foot, but it increases vision forward and to leeward, and stops chafe along the foot making the sail last longer.

The sail can now be hanked on to the forestay making sure, as the bottom hank is put on, that the luff is not twisted between it and the tack. With the first hank on, run your hand up the luff until you reach the second and put that on. Continue running your hand along the luff between each hank and the next to ensure that none is missed and that there are no twists in the luff. As each hank is put on make sure that it faces the same direction as the others and that the piston closes completely, otherwise it will come off and the sail will have to be lowered and resecured.

As you work up the luff the sail will of course all come out of its bag, but it is attached to the boat and should not be lost. Make sure that you are working from the windward side of the sail else it could smother you or even push you towards the side.

When the sail is completely hanked on put some tiers round it to keep it from blowing up the forestay or over the rail.

If the sheets are not already rove (threaded) through the lead blocks sort them out and set them up, remembering to alter the position of the blocks on their tracks if necessary and to lead them correctly either inside or outside the shrouds, and finally to put a figure of eight stopper knot in the ends at the cockpit to prevent them running out through the blocks. Take hold of the foot of the headsail at the tack and run your hand along it all the way to the clew to remove any twists. At the clew make sure the foot is below the leech. Fasten the sheets on using one of the methods discussed in the last chapter.

Finally, take the headsail halyard and make sure it is not twisted or foul and, making sure the fall is secured so that it cannot run aloft, fasten the other end to the head of the sail. This is usually done with either a captive-pin shackle or a snapshackle, both being fairly quick and easy to use. The operation of the snapshackle is made easier if a short knotted lanyard is attached to the pin. Do not use a loose pin shackle – it will be lost on a dark night when the boat is pitching in a seaway. With the halyard on, the headsail is ready for hoisting.

The falls of all halyards must be stopped from running aloft, and this is usually done by passing the bitter end through a hole in the cleat and tying a figure of eight in it. The halyard is then used as though the end were free – it is not hauled all the way through this hole when the sail is being hoisted – and is turned up on the cleat in the normal fashion. Other methods used are to attach the bitter end to a swivel on deck (or to a length of twine fastened to a fixed eye) to absorb any twist in the halyard.

We may summarize the procedures for bending sails on as follows:

*Mainsail*
1. Tie sail bag on deck.
2. Feed foot onto boom.
3. Fasten tack to boom.
4. Set up outhaul.
5. Straighten luff by running hand all the way to head.
6. Feed slides into mast or roll sail completely round boom.
7. After slides fed into mast, secure gate closed.
8. Insert battens. This must be done before rolling sail round boom if that is to be done.
9. Put tiers on.
10. Attach halyard and use to hold head down, or use tier.
11. Attach and overhaul kicking strap.
12. Attach and overhaul gooseneck downhaul if fitted.

*Headsail*
1. Tie bag to guardrail.
2. Attach tack to pennant, downhaul or stemhead fitting.
3. Overhaul tack tackle if used.

4. Hank onto forestay ensuring no twists or missed hanks.
5. Apply tier to hold sail down.
6. Set up sheets if not already done.
7. Run hand from tack to clew removing any twists.
8. Attach sheets to clew.
9. Fasten halyard to head of sail.

Bending sails on is more complicated to read about than to carry out, the important thing is to follow a pattern, a regular sequence of working that will not allow anything to be missed out. Check everything, even if you know it has all been done. The processes to be gone through are the same whether they are carried out on a quiet mooring or in half a gale at sea. The difference is in the physical aspects. At sea you will need to work on the foredeck in a kneeling or sitting position for much of the time. If you stand up, say to flick a halyard free that has wrapped itself round a spreader end, you are in great danger of being pitched off your feet by an unexpected roll of the boat. Always work from the windward side of the sail – I have repeated this several times because it is so important from a safety point of view. Never stand on a sail; it is slippery on the deck and it may be hiding an open hatch or a stowed spinnaker pole. When moving about with a bagged up sail it is far better to drag it along the deck and have one hand free to hold on with, than to take it up in your arms and fall overboard when the boat lurches. THINK SAFETY.

## Hoisting sails

The mainsail is hoisted most easily when the boat is head to wind, as there is then no pressure in the sail and there is no chance of a batten fouling the rigging. When he is ready the person hoisting the sail signals to the helmsman to bring the boat's head up into the wind. In most conditions this can be done simply with a call, but it is quieter to have a pre-arranged signal, such as a thumbs-up sign, which the helmsman will recognize.

If the sail is covered with a coat this must first be removed, rolled up and stowed away, then the tiers can be taken off, all bar one to keep the bunt of the sail under control. Whether you put all the tiers in a cockpit locker immediately or hitch them to the coachroof grabrails until the sail is set is a matter of personal preference. I usually tie them to the grabrails or round my waist to avoid an extra trip to the cockpit.

Release the mainsheet and overhaul it to be sure it can run freely, then leave it slack. The topping lift must now be set up to take the weight of the boom until the sail is hoisted and can support the weight itself. Don't let the fall of the topping lift get in the way, but don't bother to coil it up as it will be freed again shortly. If the boom was resting in a crutch this should now be unshipped and stowed, or if gallows are fitted they should be lowered to their sailing position. I would strongly advise against the use of a scissors-type boom support as it will assuredly pinch your fingers one day.

Check next that the gooseneck downhaul and kicking strap are freed off in case they were not released when the mainsail was last handed and stowed. These and the mainsheet are the things that are usually forgotten, though the mainsheet is normally noticed when the topping lift is set up. The downhaul and kicking strap only come to light when the sail will not go up to its proper position.

Remove the remaining sail tier, cast off the halyard (release the brake on a reel winch) and take up the slack in it, being extremely careful not to trap your fingers in the turns on a reel winch, but at the same time making sure none of the turns of wire overlap or are kinked, then call or signal to the helmsman to put the boat head to wind. You can start hoisting before she comes right up to the wind, but *watch the sail go up* and stop hoisting at the first sign of trouble. If you go too quickly a batten may foul on the spreaders and if you go on hoisting it will either break or tear the sail. Not good either way. While hoisting kneel down, sit or, if you must, stand with a foot braced behind you against any sudden lurch or freeing of the halyard. If the sea is rough you should have a safety harness on and, if there is a hook half way along the line, you can use the short line to brace against, thus allowing you to work with both hands in some security. Always hoist from the same side of the mast as the halyard even if it is to leeward, otherwise you will have a foul lead from the sheave making the job much harder and chafing the halyard badly. If you have to work from the leeward side, make sure you are well balanced with a foot in the scupper and perhaps a knee on the cabin top, depending on the angle of heel, but remember that the guardrails are now mainly *below* you. Keep clear of the sail as it goes up, shifting your position if necessary, so that the mast remains between you and the sail.

As the sail reaches well up the mast, take a couple of turns on the winch drum and go on hauling, then when the wire part comes to hand (if it is a wire and rope halyard) take extra turns on the drum. Never try to haul on the wire itself. About this time you will need to fit the winch handle and begin winching the sail up (with a reel winch the handle is of course used all the time during hoisting). This can either be done by one person, tailing with one hand and winching with the other, or a second person can come and work the winch while the person who has hoisted the sail tails. This avoids having to hand over the halyard and possibly letting it slip or even fly off the winch. Take more turns as necessary to keep as much of the wire on the drum as possible, passing the halyard round the winch handle very carefully so as not to let it slip and risk the handle flying round and hitting you in the face. Safer but slower is to remove the handle each time you need to add extra turns.

When the sail is hoisted as far as you want (be careful never to hoist so far that the splice in the halyard jams in the swallow of the masthead sheave) the fall is belayed and the winch handle removed. It is then either returned to the cockpit or to its stowage at the mast. On a reel winch the brake is screwed up tight and the handle removed and stowed. Remember that the last few turns of wire on a reel winch must be guided onto their separate part of the barrel away from the bulk of the wire.

The above has assumed that the boat you are on has halyard winches. If she has not, then you must hoist as far as you can and either use a tackle to set up the sail (this may take the form of a line with one end fixed and the other running through an eye or block on the end of the halyard, offering a 2:1 purchase) or you can swig it up. This involves hooking a bight of the halyard under a cleat and, while maintaining tension on the fall, pulling the halyard away from the mast at right angles then taking up the slack gained. When this has been done and the sail is well set up the fall is belayed in the usual manner.

The topping lift is next eased until it is slack and the sail supports the boom. Exactly how slack it should be can only be determined when the sail is completely set up and sheeted hard in, at which time it should just follow the curve of the leech going to windward. In other words you may well have to adjust it once under way again!

Before the boat can be put back on course and the mainsail used properly the gooseneck downhaul must be bowsed to tension the luff finally, and the kicking strap must be set up to hold the boom down. On a large boat both of these jobs are very much easier if someone can help by putting their weight on the boom.

With all this done the helmsman can bring the boat back on course, the mainsail can be sheeted in and the boat sailed, while the person who hoisted the sail tidies up the halyard fall and adjusts the topping lift if necessary.

The process for hoisting a headsail is similar. To begin with, the tiers are removed except for one to hold the bunt of the sail, and the halyard is checked for free running and then clipped on to the head of the sail. Common practice is to keep the halyard clipped onto the lug on the pulpit to which the upper guardwire is attached. It is then ready to hand when sail changing and there is no need to go aft to the mast to fetch it. A good idea is to knot the halyard either where it comes out of the mast if it is an internal halyard, or at the cleat if it is an external one, so that the clip just reaches to its securing point on the pulpit. By doing this the sail can be lowered completely, the halyard unclipped and fastened onto the pulpit without having to go aft to the mast to take up the slack and so stop it swinging about; it is already correctly tensioned.

Unlike the mainsail a headsail can be hoisted on any point of sailing, but it is easier to set up the luff with the wind forward of the beam so that the sheets can be freed enough to take the weight out of the sail. If sea conditions allow therefore, the helmsman must be ready to bring the boat up towards the wind and, if there is any question of which tack she will be on, he must let the foredeck hand know so that at this time he can move the headsail across to what will be the leeward side. Doing this ensures that the sail will lift clear and not blow across the deck either fouling on something or knocking the person over. It is as well to check also that the sheets are not pinned in tight, otherwise the sail won't be hoisted properly.

All is now ready, so the helmsman is asked to bring the boat up and, as he does so, the person at the mast removes the final tier and begins to hoist. *Watch the sail go up*, and if there is a wire pennant on the head between the sail and the halyard, hoist smartly when it has swung clear of the forestay, or it will wrap round and can be very hard to clear.

As the head of the sail nears the upper block take some turns on the winch and, if necessary, use the winch handle to finish hoisting. Like the mainsail, this can be done by one person, but a second can be a help. In a rough sea both people should try to kneel down to work, but the one working the winch may have to stand up, and he should be sure to clip on a safety harness before beginning.

Set the headsail luff up hard, but don't overdo it else the luff will carry more weight than the forestay. This often happens if it is over tightened with the boat on a run when the mast has moved forward thus easing the tension on the forestay. Where there is no winch the halyard can be set up by swigging in the manner described before, or a tack tackle (if fitted) can be used after the halyard has been belayed.

As soon as the halyard is fast the helmsman should be told and the cockpit sheet hand can begin sheeting in, so that the sail quietens down and its set can be checked. The foredeck hand makes up the fall and does any adjusting before retrieving the sail bag (if it is still on deck) and returning to the cockpit. Don't forget to remove the winch handle.

Exactly the same working and safety rules apply for setting or changing a headsail as for the mainsail: keep low on the deck, work from the windward side of the sail, hoist from the side of the mast on which the halyard is, be careful when putting extra turns on the winch not to let them all slip, and mind your fingers. The actions for hoisting the mainsail and a headsail can be summarised thus:

*Mainsail*
1. Remove sail cover/tiers (leave one).
2. Release mainsheet and overhaul.
3. Set up topping lift and remove gallows.
4. Check that downhaul and kicking strap are free.
5. Remove remaining sail tier, cast off halyard and take up slack as the helmsman brings boat to wind.
6. Hoist and watch sail go up.
7. Halyard on winch and set up as required, or swig halyard.
8. Belay.
9. Ease off topping lift.
10. Bowse down on gooseneck downhaul.
11. Set up kicking strap.
12. Make up fall.

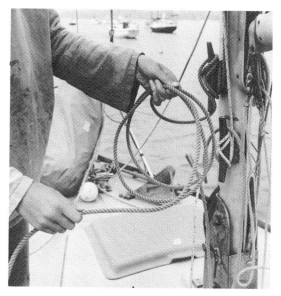
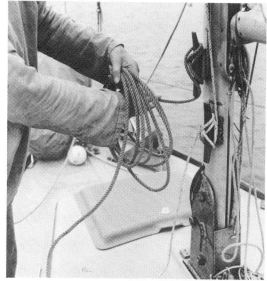
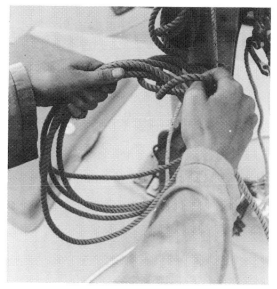

PHOTO 2

Coiling the fall of a three strand rope halyard. First a neat coil is made in the normal way, twisting the line gently with the lay so that it lies nicely, then reach through the coil and take hold close to the cleat. Pull a bight of the halyard through the coil, twist it and loop it over the upper horn of the cleat. Settle the coiled fall in place. For added security the twisted bight may be passed between the standing part of the halyard and the mast before being dropped over the cleat horn.

*Headsail*
1. Check sheets attached or run hand along foot to ensure no twists, then attach sheets and check lead.
2. Remove tiers except one.
3. Clip on halyard if not attached.
4. Move sail to leeward side of deck and ensure sheets are free.
5. Remove final tier and hoist, watching sail go up.
6. Set up halyard on winch or sweat up.
7. Belay.
8. Bowse down on tack tackle if fitted.
9. Make up fall.

All of this has supposed that the halyards are not led aft to the cockpit. If they are the hoisting is done from there, usually by another crewman, while the foredeck hand waits to see that nothing snags or fouls. Alternatively that person can return to the cockpit and hoist the sail from there. Otherwise the procedure is the same.

**Making up halyard falls**

In order that a halyard can be cast off quickly and a sail dowsed, it is important that the fall is made up so that it will not tangle and foul up. Normally, with mast-mounted cleats and rope falls, this is done by coiling the fall in loops for a laid rope and figures of eight for a core-and-sheath

type, then hanging the coils from the upper horn of the cleat. For this a bight of the halyard between the cleat and the coils is passed out through the coils, twisted with its lay and then hooked over the upper horn. The twist helps to hold all secure, but even this can be improved by passing the twisted loop behind the standing part of the halyard, between it and the mast, and then hooking it onto the horn. That way the tension in the halyard presses the loop onto the mast.

If there is more wire than will fit on the barrel of the winch, it should be passed in turns round the barrel and the cleat until the rope fall can be made up on the cleat. Never turn wire up on the cleat as this will cripple it, eventually causing some of the strands to break.

Where the winches and cleats are on the deck the method described in Chapter 3 can best be used; that is to say storing the coils under shock cord or in a trough. With reel winches there is no problem as the fall is all wound up on the barrel itself, while halyards led aft to the cockpit can best be stored there in canvas pouches or troughs.

**Trimming sails**

When the boat is first brought onto a closehauled course the headsail and mainsail should be sheeted so that each

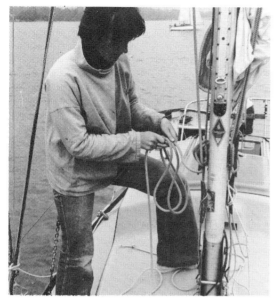

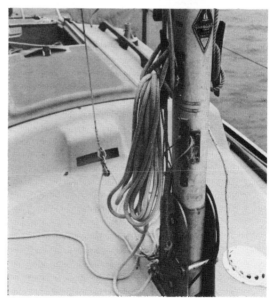

PHOTO 3
Coiling the fall of a braided halyard. Unlike a laid rope, a braided one must be coiled in figures of eight to prevent its being twisted. Once it has been coiled in this manner the process of hanging it from the upper horn of the cleat is the same as for a three strand halyard.

is drawing nicely, and the mainsail is backwinded along the luff as little as possible by the headsail. Once that is done and the boat is footing reasonably well, attention can be turned to finer trimming of each.

There is always a certain amount of twist (the fall-off of the leech from a straight line joining the end of the boom and the masthead) in a mainsail, but it should be kept to a minimum. If the sheet is simply hardened in, the lower section of the sail will no longer have a good aerofoil shape, so it is important to have a vang or kicking strap to pull the boom down. This allows the sheet to be played for maximum driving force.

The leech line of a mainsail should be kept under as little tension as possible without allowing the leech to flutter. If it is over-tightened the leech will curl to windward destroying the air flow along it.

The mainsheet traveller allows considerable control over the shape of the mainsail, particularly along its after sections. In light airs it should be brought in to the centreline of the boat so that she points well, improving her overall speed made good to windward; indeed, the traveller may be moved up to windward and the sheet eased to give the sail more flow and twist under these conditions.

As the wind picks up, it is important to ease the traveller slightly so that the boom makes an angle of around 10 degrees to the centreline, or until any tendency to hook to windward along the leech is eliminated. This also brings the traveller more directly under the boom so that twist is reduced when the sheet is hardened down. On boats without mainsheet travellers all you can do is harden down on the kicking strap as much as possible, then ease the sheet a trifle to move the boom out. Really keen types might even rig a downhaul on the boom end temporarily.

As the wind increases so will the sea, and in order to keep the boat punching through the waves rather than pitching up and down in the same hole, the mainsail must be eased and the boat freed off a few degrees. Sailing full and by like this is the only way to drive a small boat to windward in choppy seas, and is also usually much quicker in a larger boat. When the sheet is eased the traveller should be moved with it until it is as far over as it will go. By doing so the twist can still be controlled, and a guide to how much twist is permissible is given by the head of the sail. If it lifts before the lower part when the boat is luffed up slightly there is too much twist, and the sheet should be brought in a bit until the whole of the luff starts to lift at the same time.

If you keep the mainsail strapped in too tight as the wind rises it will force the bows of the boat to windward, thus increasing the amount of weather helm required to keep her on course. To counteract this the traveller should be eased and the luff tightened as far as possible with the gooseneck downhaul, but if that can't be done, and the traveller is already right out, then the sheet itself must be eased a little – in any case it may well be time to reef.

So much for going to windward, but what of reaching and running? Really this is a far easier business. On a reach it is very much a case of adjusting the trim of the sheet with the traveller moved right out, until the boat is sailing at her fastest, while on a dead run the angle of the boom to the centreline depends on how much the boom end rises and how far aft the leeward lower shroud is positioned. The boom can only be squared off until it is pressing against the leeward rigging, so on boats with lower shrouds set well aft, the boom cannot be run square off. Also if the boom lifts a lot the sail will belly forward, not only chafing badly on the shrouds as the boat rolls, but spilling air off the leech. If the boom can be held well down by the kicking strap or a downhaul, it can be run right out with little spillage, reduced chafe and increased efficiency.

The essential point about trimming the mainsail and headsail when going to windward is that the slot between them must be maintained. The curves of the two sails should run as nearly parallel as possible; the leech of the headsail and the belly of the main. This is most important as the wind increases, when the drive in the headsail will move further aft with a tendency for the leech to curl to windward, thus directing a flow of air into the leeside of the mainsail and backwinding it. If this happens it could be time to change to a smaller headsail, but the sheeting angle may also be the cause. If there is too much tension on the leech (sheet lead too far forward) it will tend to hook, while too little tension (sheet lead too far aft producing too much tension in the foot) will make it flutter. Annoying as this fluttering may be, it is less serious than a backwinded mainsail, as it will at least allow the headsail to exhaust freely and maintain the slot between it and the mainsail.

Headsails used in stronger winds, particularly storm jibs, tend to be cut with a slightly hollow leech to help keep it open, and they do not overlap the mainsail so far as a genoa – indeed a storm jib fits between the forestay and the mast, not overlapping at all. These sails should still be trimmed with some regard to the mainsail shape, but the main consideration is to keep them drawing well, and above all to prevent either leech or foot flogging. If they are allowed to flog for long in strong winds some of the seams may be started.

There is some difference of opinion as to whether the headsail should be trimmed to match the mainsail or the other way round. I suggest that they should be balanced for maximum drive, with attention being paid to which is really doing the work. This will depend in part on their relative sizes. For example, when going to windward with a No 1 genoa and a relatively small mainsail, it is the genoa that is doing most of the driving, and here it will be best to match the mainsail trim to that of the genoa.

The majority of family cruisers simply have fairlead tracks giving fore and aft adjustment for the headsail foot blocks, and do not clutter the deck with Barber Haulers and the like for athwartship adjustment of sheets. However, some boats are fitted with dual tracks giving a choice of two sheeting angles depending on the sail set and the sea conditions. Which track is used for which sails under what conditions is a matter for discussion with your sailmaker, but in general when hard on the wind a boat's pointing ability will be enhanced by closer sheeting angles. Reaching will normally require wider angles. In very light airs it may not pay to point too high and a wider sheeting angle is then desirable.

On a reach the wide sheeting base of a multihull really comes into its own, allowing a great variety of sheeting angles to be tried out. It is also possible, as we shall see later, to employ the wide base for simplifying spinnaker control.

Trimming the headsails of a cutter is not really any more complicated than trimming the sails of a sloop. All you have to do is maintain the slot between jib and staysail in the same way as between headsail and mainsail on a sloop. It is best first to set up the staysail and mainsail, then adjust the jib to match them. If the staysail is club-footed, that is to say it has a boom or club, and the sail is attached to the boom by slides, it is adjusted in the same way as a mainsail; the athwartship position of the sheet traveller on the track or horse is set to alter the sheeting angle, and the sheet is trimmed as for any other headsail. When tacking or gybing there is no adjustment necessary, it is entirely self-tending – the beauty of such an arrangement for short-handed sailing.

If the sail is only attached to the boom at the clew, then in addition to the sheet tension and athwartships positioning of the blocks, there is the additional possible adjustment of foot tension on the boom. In other words the amount of curvature in the sail can be adjusted; flatter for windward work and greater belly when freed off. When the boom has its forward end mounted on a pedestal some distance abaft the sail's tack, this adjustment of belly can also be made, but is to a certain extent taken care of for you. As the boom (and hence the sail) is freed off, so the clew is effectively brought closer to the tack, thus increasing the belly in the sail. This is arguably *the* headsail for the lazy sailor – self-tacking and self-contouring.

On a reach a ketch or yawl may set a mizzen staysail, which is really a headsail in the way it is trimmed. For a close reach it is tacked down to a point amidships and is trimmed in exactly the same manner as a proper headsail, with the mizzen playing the part of the mainsail. Going down wind it may be tacked some distance to weather to expose more of its area to the wind and bring it out from the shadow of the mizzen. If this is done, don't let it take all of the wind out of the mainsail.

### Boom guys

A boom guy or preventer is a line run from the outboard end of the boom to a point on the foredeck, and is used to brace the boom forward against the pull of the mainsheet when the boat is running or reaching. Its main purpose is to prevent an accidental gybe when on a dead run and to help hold the boom down as the boat rolls. To do this latter job it may be better to take the guy down to the deck closer to the boom so gaining

a more vertical pull, but this reduces the effectiveness of the guy in holding the boom forward.

The simplest guy, a single part rope, is set up with the boom squared off a little further than is actually required then, when the guy has been belayed, the mainsheet is hardened in drawing the boom aft to its correct position and tightening the guy. An alternative, which is no more effective, is to use a handybilly tackle enabling the guy to be set up without adjusting the trim of the mainsail, but I think this is an unnecessary complication. Another system is to lead the line aft from a snatch block on the foredeck to a cockpit cleat. By doing this a fair lead will never be achieved round the coach house, but the guy can be trimmed without going forward.

When the boat is to be gybed or tacked, the guy must be freed and eventually set up on the other side of the boat. Do not untie it from the boom, simply bring it aft from the foredeck (outside everything) and pass it across the deck abaft the mast before leading it forward on the new lee side (again outside everything). If the guy is unfastened from the boom it will need to be re-attached and that either means bringing the boom end inboard, or leaning dangerously out over the rail. To avoid this problem altogether it is sensible to keep the guy permanently attached to the boom and led forward to the mast where it can be cleated and coiled when not in use. While reefing the mainsail care must be taken not to tie or roll the line into the sail.

If a boom guy is rigged in heavy weather and there is any chance of the boom end dipping in a sea it must be slackened off somewhat to avoid either parting the line or breaking the boom.

**Team tacking and gybing**

If team sail handling is to be successful everyone must know what is going to happen, the order in which things must be done, what their particular job is and where it fits in to the sequence of events. A crew that sails together regularly and knows their boat is always recognisable, as they work smoothly and quickly with the minimum of fuss. If a new person is introduced he must be told exactly what he is to do, especially if it is blowing hard. A day of light airs when you are just 'out for a sail' rather than going anywhere or racing, is the time to practice a crew, then if things don't go quite according to plan little or no harm is done.

When tacking, the helmsman's job is to bring the boat about at a speed matched to the pace of the crew. This applies mainly to modern light displacement boats that can be spun

round; heavier, long keel boats must be sailed round and the crew must match their speed to that of the boat. The helmsman must not have the bows through the eye of the wind and falling off on the new tack while the headsail is still aback, nor must he be so slow that the crew has the headsail sheeted in on the new side before it can fill on that tack. In the first case the boat will bear away too far, and in the second she is likely to end up in irons.

When the helmsman calls 'Ready about' the crew moves into action, the sheet hands (assuming just two people) going one to each side. The one on the current leeside takes all but one turn of the sheet off its cleat so that he can still hold it without any slackening of tension, but at the same time he is ready to let fly. The other hand takes a couple of turns with the current windward sheet on its winch and takes in the slack. The helmsman's call of 'Ready about' should be answered by each man, when he is at his post, with 'Ready here'. They should now be ready for the call 'Lee-oh' as the helmsman puts the helm down. If the boat is slow in coming about he may then inform the crew 'Helm's a-lee'.

As the headsail backs and begins to shake, the hand at the leeward sheet casts the remaining turn off the cleat and all the turns off the winch, and lets the sheet fly. He must ensure that it is free to run out and, if necessary, must wait to help it before collecting the winch handle and moving to the other side of the boat. The hand on that side takes in the slack in the sheet as the headsail comes over, being careful not to get ahead of things and haul the sail aback putting the boat in irons or, worse, throwing her back on the old tack. As the boat's head passes through the eye of the wind and the sail comes over to the new lee side, the sheet hand rattles in the sheet and puts one or two more turns on the winch barrel before the sail starts to draw. If he's too slow in putting the extra turns on, the sheet will suddenly come taut and possibly trap his fingers against the barrel. When he has got in as much slack as he can unaided, the other sheet hand puts the handle in the winch and begins to wind the sail home, the first person tailing for him.

Finally, when the sail is correctly trimmed, the person tailing belays the sheet, tidies up the fall and the winchman removes and stows the winch handle. Never leave the handle in a top-action winch – or a bottom-action one if the handle is removable.

There is little to be done with a boomed or club-footed headsail as it is self-tending and simply swings across the boat and re-sets itself, like the mainsail.

The mainsheet traveller may need some adjusting for the new tack, but otherwise there is nothing to do when tacking the mainsail; gybing is a different matter.

On the command 'Stand by to gybe', the boom guy (preventer) is removed, brought aft outside everything and taken across ready to set up on the other side. A member of the crew then takes hold of the mainsheet above the cleat and either begins to haul in slowly or awaits the call 'Gybe-oh', at which exclamation the helmsman puts the helm up and the hand on the mainsheet begins to haul in quickly. As the boat's stern comes up to the wind, the boom should be over the quarter or a little further inboard. At this point if there is any weight in the wind the crewman takes a quick turn on the cleat and holds the sheet until the stern has gone through the wind and the boom has swung across. He then frees the sheet and pays it out as fast as he can. He *does not* let it run through his hands or else he will finish up with bad rope burns. During all this the sheet has remained cleated at the correct length for the run so that, if anything happens and the sheet is let go entirely, the boom cannot run right off and hit the shrouds.

In smaller boats in light winds it may not be necessary to take a snubbing turn as the boom goes across, but it is a wise precaution against rope burns even so because the real wind strength is not always appreciated when on a run. Never allow the boom to slam across intentionally from broad off on one side to broad off on the other, as the mainsheet is sure to foul up on something or even to wrap itself round someone's neck – which would be very nasty indeed. When an accidental gybe does occur you just have to duck fast and resolve in future to rig a preventer.

Although I and many others have been known to take hold of the whole mainsheet and haul it over to help the boom across, rather than haul it in as described above, this is bad practice and is likely to end up with the sheet fouled round something. Don't do it.

Once the boom is squared off on the new gybe, all that remains is for the guy to be set up as discussed in an earlier section.

If there is a whisker pole set up to boom the headsail out on the opposite side to the mainsail, it must be handed and stowed on the preparatory command 'Stand by to gybe'. One sheet hand then takes all but the final turn off the cleat and prepares to let the sheet fly, while the other person takes a turn round the winch and takes up the slack in the new sheet. They should acknowledge the helmsman's call with 'Ready here'.

At the call 'Gybe-oh', the helm is brought up and as the headsail collapses and falls in, the final turn is taken off the cleat and the turns are thrown off the winch, but the sheet as a whole is *not* let fly. Instead it is eased as the other sheet is hauled in. If the sheet were let fly the sail would blow forward and wrap itself round the forestay.

When the clew passes across the centreline of the boat and the headsail begins to fill on the new gybe, the old sheet is let go completely. More turns are taken on the new winch and the sheet is winched in and finally made up as described for tacking. Then if it is required, the whisker pole can be set up again.

In light airs a boomed headsail can be left to look after itself, but in any stronger winds it should be treated like the mainsail and sheeted in as the boat gybes, then freed off again on the new gybe.

Before a gybe it is the helmsmans' job to hold the boat steady before the wind and give the crew time to prepare. Then, when everyone is ready, he puts the helm up and brings the boat round smartly. Just as when tacking, he must meet the boat with opposite rudder to stop her falling off too far and then steady her on the new course as quickly as possible to allow the sheet hands to trim their sails correctly.

In this section we have talked only of a helmsman and two crew. With any larger number of people the cockpits of most family cruisers become too crowded for easy working. One extra person is acceptable as he or she can cope with the old leeward headsail sheet (for example) while the other two people set themselves up as a winching team, one tailing, the other grinding in on the new side. Any more than this foursome is definitely a crowd, and it may on some occasions be necessary to banish them below for the duration of a tack or gybe in order to avoid total chaos.

The procedures for tacking and gybing can be summarized as follows:

## Tacking

*Headsail*
1. 'Ready about'.
2. Take all but last turn of sheet from cleat.
3. Lay two turns on new winch and take up slack.
4. 'Lee-oh'.
5. Let fly sheet as headsail luffs.
6. Keep taking in slack in new sheet.
7. As head passes through eye of wind rattle sheet in.
8. Take extra turns on winch before sail draws.
9. Insert handle, and winch while second person tails.
10. When trimmed, belay.
11. Remove and stow handle, tidy sheet tail.

*Mainsail*
Leave alone, but adjust traveller if necessary.

## Gybing

*Headsail*
1. 'Stand by to gybe'.
2. Hand whisker pole if set.
3. Take up slack in new sheet and put two turns on winch.
4. Take all but last turn of old sheet off cleat.
5. Crew call 'Ready here'.
6. 'Gybe-oh'.
7. As sail collapses ease old sheet, haul in new.
8. When sail gybed, let fly old sheet, take extra turns on winch with new one.
9. Winch in and belay.
10. Remove handle and stow.
11. Set up whisker pole if required.

*Mainsail*
1. 'Stand by to gybe'.
2. Remove guy and pass round mast.
3. Take hold of mainsheet.
4. Crew call 'Ready here'.
5. 'Gybe-oh'.
6. Haul in sheet smartly and snub it.
7. When boom and sail have gone across pay out sheet handsomely.
8. Set up boom guy.

## Singlehanded tacking and gybing

In essence, the only difference between tacking or gybing a boat on your own and with a crew is that, when alone, you have to do all the jobs yourself. To avoid having to perform magnificent athletic feats you must be sure that you have a routine worked out in advance. It helps enormously if the boat can be made to steer herself for at least a short time, otherwise you are tied to the helm when you want to be free to concentrate on winching or some other task requiring you to move out of reach of the tiller or wheel. Most boats can sail themselves for a short time with the helm lashed, and to this end it is helpful to make up lashings that can be put on simply and quickly when needed, and can also be knocked off in a hurry.

The order of doing things is the same when singlehanded as when crewed but, before gybing or bringing the boat about, pause a moment and check that everything really is ready. The sheets are clear to run; the slack in the new sheet is taken up; the winch handle is ready (not fitted but nearby); there are no boats or other obstructions hidden behind the sails; and so on.

Tacking is the easier job since the mainsail does not have to be tended, but even so you have plenty to do. Put the helm down, let fly the old sheet, and rattle in the new one as you keep the helm over, usually with a leg or your backside, then as soon as she is round on the new tack, meet her with the rudder and either lash the helm or again hold it with some part of your body while you winch in and belay the sheet. This is all made easier by having the sheet winches and cleats within reach of the helm.

When everything is prepared and you are ready to gybe, haul in the mainsheet and belay it or at least take a snubbing turn, then shift the helm, let the boom swing across and meet the boat with the rudder. Steady her and pay out the mainsheet.

At this stage the boat will either be running dead down wind with her mainsail out on one side and her headsail on the other, that is to say wing and wing, or else the headsail will have tried to gybe and be aback, held by its old sheet.

It doesn't matter if this has happened. Only when you have gybed the mainsail and steadied the boat need you deal with gybing and sheeting in the headsail. Free the old sheet and haul in on the new, trying of course not to let the sail belly forward of the forestay in case it wraps up. Winch in the new sheet as far as necessary and belay.

All this will take longer than gybing with a crew to help, but if you follow a careful routine it can be done quite quickly and smoothly. Take it steadily though and don't get into a panic.

It is when sailing a boat singlehanded that a boomed headsail is so nice, since it can cope with itself when either tacking or gybing. The Chinese lugsail rig too is very handy indeed as nothing has to be touched when tacking, and there is no headsail to worry about when gybing. The same applies to a cat boat with its single, large sail. By the way, if sailing on a ketch or yawl, the mizzen is treated in exactly the same way as the mainsail, and if you are trying to gybe when singlehanded, it is advisable to sheet it close in and forget it until the mainsail and headsail have been dealt with. Don't forget to hand a mizzen staysail before either tacking or gybing, otherwise the main boom will do the job for you.

## Organized sail changing

Whether working as a team or singlehanded it is important when sail changing to follow a strict routine to avoid missing some vital job, or forgetting some piece of equipment, and so having to make another trip fore and aft. Remember that all the time spent moving about on deck is time spent at risk so there should be no hanging about once you leave the cockpit. That doesn't mean you should rush things, but work steadily and as fast as you safely can.

In earlier sections we looked in detail at procedures for bending on and hoisting headsails, and later on we will do the same for handing them. Changing headsails involves both these routines and a few moments spent in the cockpit thinking out the steps to be taken will be well worthwhile. If there are two of you going forward in rough weather, decide your individual tasks and if necessary arrange signals to the helmsman or another crew member in the cockpit. Then collect any gear you will need such as winch handle, sail tiers and shackle key (though shackles requiring keys to undo the pins are not recommended) before moving up forward.

The main decision when allotting tasks is who will work at the mast (assuming that's where the halyards are) and who will actually handle the sails in the bows. The cockpit crew (or helmsman) will have to handle the sheets so that decision is already made. The halyard person will lower one sail and hoist the next, and be responsible for swopping the sheets from the old sail to the new. He may also take the old sail from the bow man and send it below while the new one is being hanked on. The bow man for his part will dowse the old sail, unhank it and either bag it up with the help of the halyard man, or give it to him to be sent below. He will then hank on the new sail, sort out and pass the clew to the halyard man so he can bend on the sheets, clip on the halyard and watch the sail go up and set clear.

When singlehanded or at least with only a helmsman and one foredeck hand you will either have to adjust the sheets to look after themselves, or the helmsman will have to cope with them. On the foredeck you will have to do all the work yourself, so it is even more important than usual to keep to a routine to avoid mistakes and omissions. Think it all out in advance and then stick to your plan.

Sail changing on a multihull, particularly a lightweight racing cat or tri is best done with the boat stopped. Because of her lightness and speed it is very easy for the boat to flick a person off the foredeck and overboard. The little time lost by stopping is soon made up and the increased safety is well worthwhile. Heavier cruising catamarans may be sailed on in a subdued manner but, even with a light monohull, it is sensible to consider taking the way right off for a few minutes in rough going.

## Moving about with sail bags

Even a moderate size sail bag is a cumbersome thing to carry to or from the foredeck, and one for a large genoa is potentially a very awkward customer.

The obvious answer is to keep the sail bags in the forepeak of the boat and bring them on deck or send them below through the forehatch, but for many of the smaller stock boats this is impractical as the forecabin is used as a sleeping area and there is no room for sail stowage. On such boats you are left with moving fore and aft with an unwieldy bag.

I have found the best way of taking a sail bag along the deck is to tuck it under one arm if it is small enough and walk backwards or sideways. With a bigger bag I drag it along. It sounds a bit odd and probably looks it, but if you heave a large bag up in your arms and try to walk facing forward you cannot see where you are placing your feet. Finding a good foothold, or handhold, becomes a matter of luck–and luck is not a reliable safety aid.

Whatever method you adopt, use only one hand, the other *must* be available for holding on. In rough weather sit down and slide sideways on your backside. Crawl if necessary, just remember that if you pick up a weighty bag and it catches on say a stanchion it will throw you off balance and you can be overboard in a trice, or if you are moving aft through the cabin and take a tumble you could injure yourself.

## Sail stowages

All too often designers and builders of small family cruisers seem to ignore the fact that the boat will be equipped with sails that need to be stowed away when not in use. The fact is that even the smallest boat will need stowage for at least a couple of headsails, and more likely three if one is not to live on the forestay. The only boats for which this will not be true are those rigged with Chinese lugsails (junk rig), and those fitted with roller reefing headsails, both of which we will return to when discussing reefing. So what do we do with bagged up sails?

The commonest stowages are in cockpit lockers or in the forecabin. The cockpit lockers must have wide enough openings and be sufficiently deep to accommodate all the bags without a lot of pushing and heaving. It is hopeless piling the bags up one on top of the next because at some time, usually when it is rough and wet, you will want to get the bottom-most bag out (inevitably the storm jib), and that will mean taking out all the ones above it and littering them about the cockpit. The best way of stowing the bags is vertically, side by side, with a clear marking on top to indicate which sail is in which bag. Don't use codes for this, just plain words, like 'Storm jib' or 'No 2 genoa', then there will be no confusion.

The usual alternative to cockpit stowage is to dump all the sail bags on the forecabin bunks. This may be all right if no one is using the berths, but if you take extra crew, what will you do with the sail bags then? If you insist on using the forecabin for sail stowage, lay the bags athwart the bunks, tops pointing inboard so that you can read the labels; if they are laid fore and aft they will roll off onto the sole. Rigging leecloths on the bunks helps to form mangers that will hold the bags in place.

On a large boat where the accommodation can be arranged so that there are no bunks in the forepeak (which is, after all, an uncomfortable place to sleep at sea and one that is often completely untenable in heavy weather), it is worth considering devoting the space to sail stowage in the form of a series of bins. The sailbags can be dropped straight into these bins when they come down through the forehatch, and there is thus no problem of them ending up in a jumbled heap, or of finding the required sail. Don't forget if you do propose to pass sails through the forehatch that they must be bagged up small enough to go through without too much of a struggle.

A few people choose to keep sails on deck all the time, either bagged up and lashed down (usually under an upturned dinghy), or in 'sail sausages'. These are sailcloth tubes laced down to the toerail, into which the headsail is put when it is unhanked from the forestay; they are closed with either Velcro or a zip. This is not a common system, but it has the merit of avoiding the need to shift bagged up sails along the deck or manhandling them from below.

One idea that has possibilities, particularly on a specialized singlehanded boat, is building a series of sail bins into the foredeck. Each would have a separate watertight hatch so that the sail can be dropped straight in and the hatch closed. No one that I know of has yet tried it and there are probably some unsuspected drawbacks, but it might be worth thinking about.

## Handing and stowing sail

The most difficult thing when handing sail is to keep control and avoid letting the sail fill with wind and either go overboard or push you over. To stop this latter event, it is essential to haul down the sail from its windward side, when if anything goes wrong it will blow away from you rather than smothering you or bellying up under you as it would if you worked from the leeward side.

As with hanking on and setting sail it is wise when handing to follow a set routine that will avoid delays and extra work whether it is dark, light, blowing or a flat calm. Start by not leaving the cockpit until

you have sorted out exactly what you are going to do and what you are going to require in the way of winch handles, sail tiers or shackle spanners. A quick discussion with the helmsman can also make life easier. Decide whether he will luff up to take the wind out of the sail being handed (for instance the mainsail) or whether he will bear away to put the headsail in the lee of the mainsail. Sort out at what point the sheets will need freeing or hardening in, and what signals will be used. Much of this will only need discussion once to establish the routine and will thereafter be a matter of course, but it needs to be talked over sometime.

Taking the mainsail first, remove the halyard coil from its cleat and lay it on deck with the working part on top so that it is free to run when let go. If there is a chance that it is tangled, re-coil it and then lay it down. It might even be better to flake it down in a heap rather than coil it, but this will vary with individual halyards and must be discovered by experiment. Where a reel halyard winch is fitted, the procedure is to take the weight of the halyard on the handle, release the ratchet, engage the brake and then *remove the handle* holding the weight of the sail on the brake. Never lower the sail with the handle still in the winch: it will whirl round in a lethal fashion.

With the halyard now ready to be cast

PHOTO 4
Dropping mainsail on approach to marina. Sail tiers
round waist, kneel at mast and lay out halyard.
Lower sail and bundle on top of boom as latter is
hauled in. Never lean outboard to secure sail.

off, signal to the helmsman that you are all set, then when he gives the go ahead, set up the topping lift, asking for the sheet to be freed if necessary. The helmsman luffs up or frees the sheet completely so that the wind is spilt from the sail, and then you cast off the halyard or release the brake on the winch as soon as the sail starts to shake and 'fist' the sail down *from the windward side*.

As soon as the bulk of the sail is down the mainsheet must be hardened in to avoid the sail going in the water and to facilitate its being smothered and secured. Cleat the sheet securely so that the person on deck can lean his full weight against it in safety.

Haul the mainsail down near the luff and actually use the luff rope or tape if the slides are sticky, but don't keep on heaving when something jams or you will damage the sail. Stop and find out what the trouble is – very often a tangle in the halyard – sort it out and then go on hauling down. Don't pull down on the leech as you will stretch it out of shape.

When the mainsail is completely down you must work quickly to secure it and stop it flogging about. Only a rough stow is required immediately, but it is best achieved by forming a trough with the bottom few feet of sail rolling the rest of the canvas into it then lashing the sausage so formed on top of the boom. Sail tiers should either have been brought on deck

with you or they should be hitched ready onto the coachroof grabrails. I prefer to keep them hitched on the grabrails, but if you would rather bring them on deck with you, it is better to tie them individually round your waist than stuff a bundle in your pocket. With a bundle in the pocket it is almost impossible to pull one tie out without the rest coming with it and blowing away.

Once two or three tiers have been put round the sail sausage, dip a bight of the halyard under the bottom horn of its cleat, set it up taut and cleat the fall. This pulls the head of the sail down to stop it rising up the mast again and tidies up the fall of the halyard in one go. Don't haul the head down too hard however or it will be damaged at the top slide. The bitter end of the halyard must remain secured at all times so that it is not lost up the mast when the halyard is uncleated.

Finally the boom is lowered into the gallows if any are used and the mainsheet is overhauled and coiled. The kicking strap and boom downhaul are also overhauled ready for the mainsail to be re-set.

Gaff mainsails are treated similarly, but they are pushed down by the weight of the gaff and should not have to be hauled down. Both throat and peak halyard must be eased, but normally the peak halyard is checked away until the gaff is horizontal, and they are then eased together so that the gaff remains horizontal.

Although they fell from popularity with athe dvent of the small mainsail/large headsail rig, it is still a great help when handling a mainsail on your own if a set of lazyjacks is rigged. These take the form of twin topping lifts, one each side of the boom, with secondary lines passing in loops under the boom and connecting them together. As the sail is lowered it is held between the lazyjacks and cannot blow about out of control; a gaff too can be controlled in this way. One rig that still uses them to good effect is the Chinese lugsail where the sail self-stows between them. The halyard is eased (normally without anyone having to leave the cockpit as it is led aft) and each batten lays itself neatly on top of the lower one between the lazyjacks, and finally the yard rests on top of them all to hold them down. Very neat, very simple.

When the mainsail has been lowered and secured to the boom as described you must either pass more gaskets to make sure it doesn't blow loose, or you must make a harbour stow of it. This means stowing it in the same fashion, but considerably more neatly. Form the same trough in the foot of the sail and flake the rest of the sail into it, pulling out towards the leech as much as you can to straighten the cloth. Fold the trough over and roll it tightly down onto the top of the boom,

securing it with several sail tiers so that it forms a neat, tight roll.

A gaff mainsail is dealt with slightly differently in that the sail is furled between boom and gaff by hauling the leech forward instead of aft. The bunt of cloth is pulled out from between the spars and, with the leech held forward, it is rolled up into a trough made with the foot. The sausage formed is then secured between the spars with tiers and the spars are themselves lashed together. If the sail is loose footed the bundle is secured to the gaff rather than the boom.

Headsails are generally harder to control when setting or handing than mainsails, because they are only attached along one edge, leaving the rest of the sail free to flog about and cause trouble. The aim therefore must be to muzzle the sail as fast as possible, and it is particularly important with a headsail to remember to work from the windward side and to haul it down from the foot rather than try to get on top and push it down. It's all too easy for it to fill with wind and belly up under you. Netting, or a light line zig-zagged between the upper guardwire and the toerail from shrouds to pulpit on each bow, will help enormously in keeping the sails out of the water after they have been handed.

As with any deck work, don't leave the cockpit until you have sorted out what you are going to do. A light multihull may

PHOTO 5
Handing genoa. With a number of sail tiers round waist, sort out and cast off halyard. Haul sail down from kneeling or sitting position on deck, trying to keep the sail inboard of the guardrails. Unclip halyard from sail and attach to pulpit for security. Set up halyard if necessary then tie sail down.

have to be stopped to allow safe sail handling, while foredeck work on a monohull is far simpler if the boat is turned off downwind, bringing the headsail into the lee of the mainsail, than if she is kept driving to windward. Decide with the helmsman what approach is to be taken and what signals will be made. Gather together any tiers and tools you will require, then move forward to the mast where the first job is to lay the halyard coil on deck or flake it down with the working part on top so that there is no chance of its fouling up as the sail is brought down.

When you are ready, signal the fact to the helmsman and, as he either bears away so that the headsail comes into the lee of the mainsail, or the sheet is started to spill the wind from the sail, cast off the halyard and start gathering it in. Unless you're in a flat calm it is usually best to sit on deck and pull the sail into your lap. In this position you are safe and the sail is brought down inside the guardrails. If you stand up to work, particularly if you reach up to the sail, it only takes a lurch of the boat to throw you off balance, or for you to step on some of the sailcloth and slip, or the sail to belly up under you and you are in serious trouble.

As the bulk of the sail comes down the clew will try to go over the rail into the sea, but it can be prevented if the sheet is hardened in to draw the clew aft along the sidedeck. The timing here must be right or the tension on the sheet will prevent the hanks sliding down the forestay. Wait until the clew is down to the level of the rail and then harden in the sheet.

Once the sail is down on deck it must be secured quickly by passing tiers round it and one guardwire. This serves the double purpose of preventing it from blowing about, and holds the furled sail in one place so that it can't get in the way of other foredeck work such as mooring or anchoring. I like to keep a couple of tiers hitched onto the guardwire for just this purpose. They may not look very pretty but they are instantly to hand and all that has to be done is to pass the ends round the bundle of sail and tie them together. The tier itself is already attached to the guardwire.

The head of the sail must be held down with a tier to stop it blowing back up the forestay, and the halyard can either be left clipped on ready for re-hoisting (in which case it can be used instead of a tier to hold the head down to the pulpit), or it can be undone and clipped onto a strong point on the pulpit such as a terminal loop for the guardrails. A trip back to the mast can be saved by knotting the fall (as described earlier in this chapter) so that the halyard is in tension as you clip it onto the pulpit. Otherwise you have to clip it onto the pulpit, rush back to the mast before the halyard gets fouled up aloft, and set it up tight.

With the sail safely on deck the boat can be put back on course while a tidier stow is made, but if time is not pressing it is safer and more comfortable for the foredeck hand if the boat is kept before the wind until he has finished and returned aft.

If the boat is being anchored or moored for the night, a mainsail cover may be put on over the stowed sail to keep it clean and protect it from ultra violet radiation (which is harmful to synthetic cloth over a period of time). The headsail, if it is not to be removed altogether, may be fed into its sailbag while still attached to the forestay. The sheets are led out of the mouth of the bag which is drawn up round the hanks and hitched to the stay.

Exactly the same procedures are used at night, but more than ever it is important to cease hauling on the sails if something jams, and always follow the same pattern of working, right down to moving the halyard to or from the head of a sail along the same path to ensure it does not get fouled up.

Where a jib is set on a bowsprit without the benefit of a tack traveller or roller furling gear, it is worth using a downhaul running from the head through a block on the bowsprit and aft to the mast. The halyard is eased as the downhaul is brought in and, if the sheet is hardened in, the jib is kept under complete control and only needs a couple of gaskets to keep it secure along the bowsprit.

The procedures for handing mainsail and headsail can be summarized thus:

*Mainsail*
1. Overhaul halyard fall and lay out on deck.
2. Set up the topping lift (sheet may need easing).
3. Luff or free the mainsheet to spill wind.
4. Cast off halyard and haul sail down by luff.
5. Harden in mainsheet and belay.
6. Rough stow with 2-3 tiers.
7. Hold head down with halyard under cleat.
8. Settle boom in gallows if used.
9. Overhaul and coil mainsheet, kicking strap and downhaul.
10. Harbour stow or extra tiers.

*Headsail*
1. Overhaul halyard and flake down on deck.
2. Let fly sheet or turn down wind.
3. Cast off halyard and haul down at luff.
4. Harden in sheet to keep sail out of water.
5. Tiers.
6. Secure head and halyard.
7. Stow sail more tidily or remove.
8. Return to original course.

## Reefing systems

Mainsail reefing systems generally fall into two categories: roller reefing and slab reefing. In a roller reefing system the mainsail is rolled round the boom to reduce its area. This is done by removing the kicking strap (which is discarded unless it is on a boom claw or has a canvas strop that can be rolled into the sail), slackening the halyard and operating a worm gear at the gooseneck to revolve the boom. A neater roll is achieved if someone can haul the leech out along the boom, but this is not always possible. The drawbacks to this system are that the mainsail slides have to be removed from their track as they reach the bottom of it and, all too often, the further the sail is rolled up, the more the boom end droops until it eventually hits the heads of the crew in the cockpit or fouls the mainhatch. The second problem can be avoided with a boom that is fatter or has shaped wedges fitted at its outboard end, and by using a sail with a tape luff rather than a roped one, but all too few boats are so equipped.

Sometimes the worm gear on the boom is replaced by a direct drive system through the mast (called 'through mast reefing') where one turn of the handle produces one revolution of the boom. This allows the boom to be revolved faster but has no great advantage otherwise. It is usually used on sails where the bolt rope feeds into a groove in the mast rather than being attached to slides. When the sail is lowered it comes free from the mast (unlike a sail attached to slides running in a track or groove) and most people stow it by rolling it round the boom. It looks neat but often hoisting is difficult unless a special luff feeder is fitted or someone can feed the bolt rope back into the mast while another person hoists. More trouble comes when the sail is dropped in a hurry, because it spreads all over the deck.

When a roller reefed mainsail is to have the reef shaken out the worm gear is turned the other way, the slides (or bolt rope) are fed back into the track, and the sail is hoisted as it is unrolled from the boom. The halyard is set up, the downhaul tightened and the kicking strap re-instated.

The other common reefing system is slab or jiffy reefing in which a cringle set in the luff of the sail is slipped over a hook in the gooseneck, and a cringle in the leech is held down to the boom by a line running from one side of the boom, through the cringle to a block on the other side of the boom and thence forward to the mast. The bunt of the sail is gathered and secured along the boom either by conventional reef points or a continuous line woven in and out of eyelets across the sail and held down by

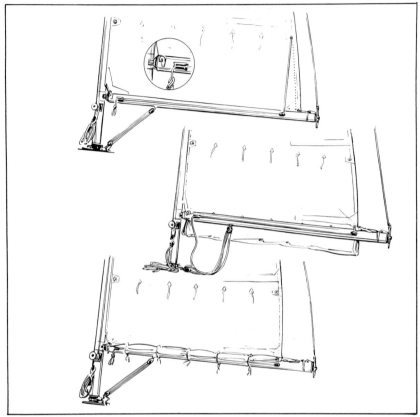

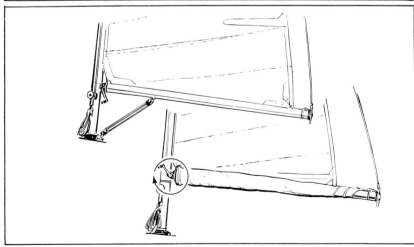

hooks on each side of the boom. The slight variation, known as jiffy reefing, omits (or delays) the gathering and securing of the bunt of cloth, making use of the inherent strength of polyester sailcloth to create a new foot.

There are two schools of thought on how to take in a slab reef. In one system a winch under the boom near the gooseneck is used to haul in the leech pennant which raises the boom to the leech cringle. The halyard is then eased, the luff cringle hooked on and the leech pennant hardened right in. The halyard is then set up again together with the kicking strap and any downhaul. The other system does away with the need for the winch. In this method the topping lift is first set up to take the weight of the boom, then the halyard is eased, the luff

FIG. 2
Slab and roller reefing systems. Before taking in a slab reef the kicking strap is released and the topping lift is set up to take the weight of the boom. The halyard is then eased and the luff cringle hooked down to the boom. The leech pennant is hauled in to bring the leech cringle hard down and the halyard is set up, the topping lift eased and the kicking strap hardened. The boat can then be sailed quietly while the bunt of the sail is tied up to the boom. In roller reefing systems the kicking strap is removed entirely (although a claw or fabric strop is sometimes fitted to allow its use after a reef has been taken in). The halyard is eased and the handle is turned to rotate the boom and roll up the sail. A better reef is achieved if someone can pull the leech out along the boom as the sail is rolled up.

cringle hooked on and the slack leech pennant hardened in by hand. The winch is not required because you are not having to lift the weight of the boom. Finally the halyard is retensioned, the topping lift eased, and the kicking strap and downhaul adjusted. In both methods the loose canvas need only be bundled up and secured after the sail is again in full use.

A lot of people have played around with slab reefing systems and worked out ways and means of operating the whole thing from the cockpit by leading halyards and pennants aft. This is sensible as it avoids the need to go on deck other than to tidy up the loose bunt of sail; on the other hand the method is so quick and easy to use anyway that I am not sure it is worth the extra blocks, lines and winches. It has also been arranged so that one can use a running line rather than a crank to operate a through mast gear to turn the boom for roller reefing. This set up also provides a way of reefing the main without leaving the cockpit. From this point of view there is really nothing as yet to beat the simplicity of the Chinese lugsail, where reefing is carried out just by easing the halyard and lowering one batten onto the next.

On boats with a split rig such as a ketch or yawl, reefing can well be achieved by just dropping the mainsail and continuing under mizzen and headsail, while with a cutter the first reef may be effected by handing one of the headsails.

Normally headsails are not reefed but exchanged for smaller sails, however there are now some very good roller reefing systems on the market. With modern sailcloths which are both light and strong, it is worth considering one of these or instead putting a row of reef points in an ordinary headsail. Taking this latter system first, all you need to do is partially lower the sail, move the tack fitting to a cringle higher up the luff, move the sheets to a cringle above the clew and tie in the reef points before rehoisting. Naturally it would still be wise to carry a storm jib for really bad weather, but being able to reef a medium sized genoa and create a smaller, handier sail without going through the whole unhanking, bagging up, hanking on process is certainly an advantage.

It is important when talking about headsails not to confuse roller reefing with roller furling. With roller reefing gear the sail is rolled on a luff spar and can be used with any amount rolled away or set, but with roller furling gear the sail is rolled around its own luff wire and is either all set or all stowed. On no account should you use a roller furling system to reef a headsail – you will destroy the shape of the sail.

Both reefing and furling gears are operated from the cockpit by a line wound on a drum at the tack of the sail. As the sheet is eased and the line pulled the luff spar (or wire) revolves and winds up the sail. If the line is eased and the sheet pulled the sail unfurls. It is all very simple.

Roller reefing headsails are often criticized for their poor set, but this can usually be improved by better sheeting angles or having the sail re-cut. The other bogey is breakdown of the roller mechanism, and the only answer to this is to satisfy yourself that the one you fit is man enough for the job, and to make sure that you look after it. They are well engineered fittings and failure is rare. It can happen though and it is wise to carry at least a storm jib to get you home. This should have strings of parrel beads in place of hanks to allow it to run up and down over the furled sail.

**Spinnakers**

A spinnaker, while being a beautiful sight if set properly, is an immensely powerful sail with a sinister reputation. Photographs and stories abound of boats broaching to under spinnakers and of crews struggling to unravel ones that have wrapped themselves round the forestay. This unruly behaviour tends to occur when the sail has not been sorted out properly before being set, or when an

| | | |
|---|---|---|
| Head<br>Leech — Leech<br>Clew — Clew<br>Foot<br>**SPINNAKER<br>BEFORE HOISTING** | Head<br>Leech<br>Clew<br>Luff — Sheet<br>Tack — Guy<br>**PORT GYBE** | Head<br>Luff<br>Tack<br>Guy<br>Leech<br>Clew — Sheet<br>**STARBOARD GYBE** |
| **SINGLE** | **POLE** | **GYBE** |
| **DIP** | **POLE** | **GYBE** |
| **TWIN** | **POLE** | **GYBE** |

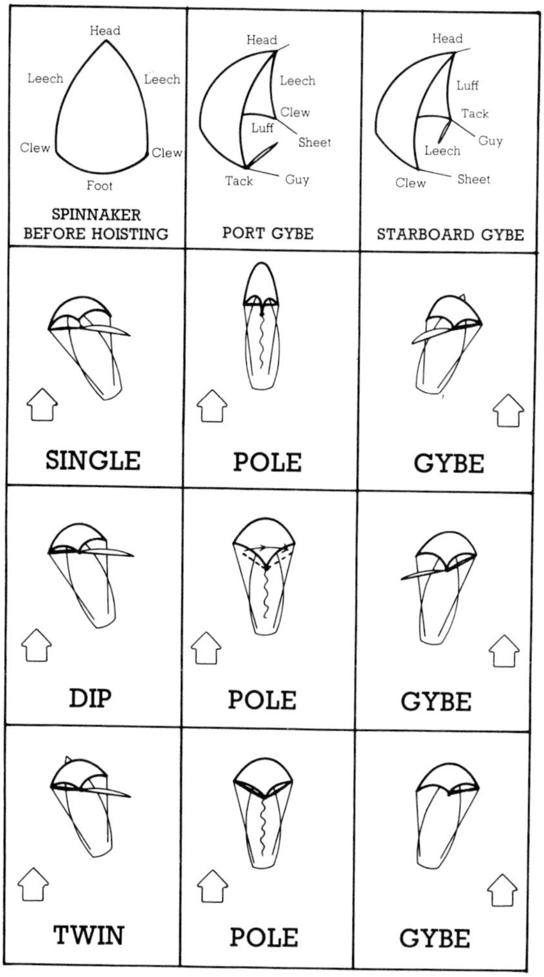

FIG. 3
The changing names given to the parts of a spinnaker and three methods of gybing.

inexperienced crew is flying the sail in too much wind. However they are not easy sails to handle, even for experts, as they spread a huge area of cloth to the wind and are only controlled at their three corners, but there is no doubt they will pull a boat down wind like nothing else.

Like any other sail a spinnaker has a head, tack, clew, foot, luff and leech, but some of the names change at times. Before the sail is set both sides are termed the leech and both bottom corners are the clews. When the sail is set the corner attached to the spinnaker pole and guy is the tack, its side is the luff, and the other corner with the sheet is the clew, its side being the leech. When the boat is gybed the pole is shifted to the other bottom corner and all the names swap over. The old luff becomes the leech, the old clew the tack, the sheet the guy. The head fortunately is always the head and the foot remains the foot.

Before setting the spinnaker it is either folded carefully and put into a turtle with the head and both clews sticking out, or it is folded into a long sausage and stopped with rubber bands. There are also easy handling devices called the Spee Squeezer or Spinnaker Sally which we will come to later.

PHOTO 6
Setting a spinnaker on a small cruiser/racer. Lash the sail bag or turtle in the pulpit, attach the sheet, guy and halyard. Set up the pole with its topping lift and downhaul and clip end to guy. Hoist sail and begin to harden in sheet and guy. Square up pole, trim sheet and guy to put luff to sleep – here it is still lifting.

A spinnaker turtle is basically a canvas bag lashed on deck from which the sail is set. The sail is gathered along each edge so that nothing is twisted, and the foot and belly are placed in the turtle. The rest of the sail is flaked down on top with the head uppermost. Three flaps fold in on top, with the head and both clews sticking out between them. When the sail is to be set the turtle is carried up on deck, the halyard and sheets attached, the turtle opened, and there's the sail all ready for hoisting.

If the sail is to be stopped with elastic bands, these are loaded onto a bucket with the bottom cut out. The sail is then pulled head first through the bucket and a band slipped off onto the sail at regular intervals. When the spinnaker is hoisted, it goes up as a sausage and, when the sheet and guy are hardened in, the wind fills the sail breaking the bands as it does so.

Before hoisting the spinnaker, the pole is set up on the windward side by clipping the heel to a fitting on the forward side of the mast and hoisting on a topping lift; a downhaul is used to stop it rising too far when the spinnaker fills. The guy runs through a fitting on the outboard end of the pole and is led right aft outside everything to a quarter block and a winch by the cockpit. The sheet is led from a quarter block and winch on the other side of the boat, forward outside all

to the foredeck, where it attaches to the clew of the spinnaker. The guy is brought round the forestay and attached to what will become the tack. The halyard, which runs through a sheave in a rotating masthead crane to keep it clear of other halyards and the forestay, is brought down to leeward of the forestay and clipped on to the head of the sail.

It is normal to hoist the spinnaker in the lee of the mainsail so that there is some chance of getting it right up before it fills and makes hoisting hard work. Should it fill too soon the halyard could well rip out of the hands of the person trying to hoist the sail, so if this is your job, keep your fingers well clear of the winch.

When everything is set up, the spinnaker is hoisted smartly and, as soon as the halyard is turned up, the guy and sheet are brought home and trimmed. If the sail was hoisted in stops this action will break it open, and the sooner it is done in any case the better as it reduces the chances of a twist developing.

As a basic guide, the spinnaker pole should be in line with the main boom, roughly at 90 degrees to the apparent wind, and once it is there the guy may be secured leaving the crew free to trim the sheet. This must be done constantly to keep the sail drawing at its best. Ease the sheet until the luff just begins to lift and curl, then sheet in a fraction and repeat. Don't ease too far or the sail will collapse, but then again don't over sheet it or it will lose drive.

The boom must be trimmed whenever the wind shifts or the boat's heading changes. Keep it more or less at right angles to the wind and adjust its height so that the tack is always on a level with the clew, thus maintaining symmetry of the sail and achieving maximum spread of the foot. If the fitting on the mast at the heel of the spinnaker pole is on a track, it should be moved up or down as appropriate to keep the heel level with the tack and the pole at right angles to the mast.

Eventually the wind is going to shift or your course is going to change and the spinnaker will have to be gybed. There are many different ways of doing this dependent upon sail area, boat size and crew ability. Where the sail area is fairly small and the rig is the simplest possible (which is the only situation I am discussing here), it is not too difficult an operation if the timing works out, but there are still three methods to describe.

The first method, which is only used with small sails, involves a short period of time when the pole is attached to both clews but not the mast, which could be nasty if the sail fills suddenly. The idea is to unclip the heel from the mast, attach it to the other clew so that both ends are on the sail, then gybe the mainsail, disconnect the pole from the old clew and attach the new free end of the pole to the mast.

For the second method the pole must either be short enough to dip across the boat inside the forestay with the heel still attached at the mast, or the heel must be on a track so that it can be slid up the mast thus allowing the pole to be dipped across. The pole is unclipped from the guy and dipped across inside the forestay as the mainsail is gybed. The pole is then clipped onto the new guy on the new weather side. To make this easier it is usual to have a line fixed to the pole which operates the two end fittings.

The third gybing method calls for the use of twin spinnaker poles and is particularly suited to short handed boats. The second pole is set up in the lee of the mainsail and is clipped onto a lazy guy, the mainsail is gybed and the old pole is unclipped and stowed. Unfortunately this method does require two poles and twice the normal amount of running rigging.

After setting a spinnaker, the thing that worries people most is the prospect of having to hand it in a squall. Admittedly things can go wrong, but if the crew can work as a team all should usually be well.

Bring the wind dead astern and ease the guy so that the pole swings right forward to the forestay. This puts the spinnaker in the lee of the mainsail and takes the drive out of it. Now the crew must work together. The guy is either let

PHOTO 7

Gybing a spinnaker by turning the pole end-for-end in a small cruiser/racer in light airs. Ease sheet and guy, unclip the pole from the mast. Clip pole onto old sheet so that it is now free of boat and attached at both ends to the spinnaker. Free the pole from the old guy and push pole out on new side. Gybe the mainsail and clip the pole onto the mast. Set pole up and trim new sheet and guy.

run so that the spinnaker flags out to leeward trailing the guy, or the tack is tripped from the guy and the sail flogs on its own. Either way the halyard is eased and, as the sail is lowered, the clew is hauled down into the cockpit or companionway. The halyard must be eased at *exactly* the rate the person handing the sail is working. Too fast and the whole lot can end up in the sea; too slow and the man handing the sail will be struggling against the halyard. When the sail is gathered, the halyard is unfastened from the head and made up at the mast. The sheet and guy are coiled away and the pole is brought in and stowed. If the spinnaker was brought down in the cockpit it must be bundled below before the wind gets into it.

The great beam of a multihull, particularly a trimaran, when compared with a monohull of the same length, offers some interesting alternatives for sailing with the wind free. In the first place a headsail may have its tack shifted out from the normal centreline position to the stem of the windward float or hull, thus presenting a much larger area of the sail to clear air. Secondly, when flying a spinnaker, you have the choice of using a pole or not as you please. This again applies more readily to a trimaran than a cat because of the greater beam, but it is possible to do without a pole on either.

Working without the spinnaker pole requires a flatter cut sail than would otherwise be used. Instead of fastening the tack to the end of the spinnaker pole the guy is led down to a block on the stem of the windward outrigger, while the sheet is led in the normal fashion to a block on the quarter of the leeward float. This gives an excellent spread to the sail and retains greater control than is achieved with a pole.

To facilitate gybing, a sheet is run from the tack to a block on the windward quarter and a guy is led from the clew to a block on the stem of the leeward float. With this set up the mainsail swings across, the old guy is eased as the new sheet is brought home, and the old sheet is eased as the new guy comes in. No foredeck work, no humping unwieldy poles about the place. Much safer.

One of the more unfortunate traits of the spinnaker is that it likes to wrap itself snugly round the forestay, particularly when it is allowed to collapse in light airs. There are other nasty habits, but this one is prevalent. It can be avoided by hoisting a special net on the forestay in place of a headsail, but for those who do not use a spinnaker sufficiently often to justify the cost of one of these nets it may be necessary instead to set up a temporary inner forestay. This might run from the hounds down to a foredeck cleat just abaft the forestay. It is not a complete antidote, but will help. A third suggestion is to hoist a storm jib under the spinnaker, but this may hinder an inexperienced crew's handling of the spinnaker itself.

The extra halyard, topping lift and downhaul required to set a spinnaker can be a headache when not in use, as some modern boats simply do not have enough mast cleats to take them all. Both parts of the halyard can be taken forward and secured to the pulpit to get them out of the way, leaving the lifts and downhauls, which may be dealt with by fitting a pin rail across the shrouds just inside the top guardwire. If so positioned it is not unsightly and can also be used for belaying the flag halyards.

Finally we come to the Spee Squeezer or Spinnaker Sally. These are similar amazing devices for simplifying spinnaker handling. Provided that you don't go beserk and start trying to set the kite in a Force 6 with just your wife and two kids on board, it will take the worry out of setting and handling the sail.

The spinnaker lives inside a light sailcloth sausage or a series of nylon rings with a specially shaped plastic bell mouth at the lower end (from which the clews project), and a swivel (with the head of the spinnaker attached) and curved stainless steel tube at the head. An endless line runs from the bell mouth up inside the sausage, out through the stainless steel tube and down again to the outside of the bell.

To prepare for setting the spinnaker the pole is clipped onto the mast and set up in approximately the right position, ie at 90 degrees to the wind and at right angles to the mast. The sheet is led from aft outside everything and clipped onto the clew of the spinnaker. The guy is led similarly outside everything, through the end fitting of the pole, round the forestay, and is clipped onto the tack of the sail. The halyard is fastened to the swivel at the head of the sausage, making sure that there is no twist in a white tape line stitched down the after side of the Squeezer.

To set the spinnaker the Squeezer, with the spinnaker inside, is hoisted and the halyard belayed. The continuous line is hauled on to raise the bell mouth and, as it goes up, the sheet and guy are hardened in. As soon as the wind begins to get into the foot of the sail a turn must be taken round a foredeck cleat with the downhaul on the bell, so that it can be surged against the force of the wind opening the sail and lifting the bell. If this is not done the bell will spring up and the sail will open with a bang; if the line is surged the sail can blossom in a totally controlled manner at whatever speed you choose.

The beauty of the system is that the sail is hoisted completely and the halyard secured before the wind can ever get

PHOTO 8
Setting a spinnaker on a 32-footer with the help of a
Spee Squeezer can be a smooth, controlled
operation. The pole is set up, the Spee Squeezer is
hoisted with halyard, sheet and guy attached to the
spinnaker inside it and with care being taken to keep
the white guideline untwisted. The bell of the
Squeezer is first hoisted and then surged upwards
while the sheet and guy are trimmed. Finally the
whole spinnaker blossoms with the bunched up
Squeezer resting above its head.

into the sail and, as the sail is broken out in such a controlled fashion a wrap is unlikely to happen, though one could of course occur after the sail is set and trimmed.

The bell of the Spee Squeezer sits above the head of the spinnaker and does not interfere with it in any way. The sail is gybed in the normal manner but, if you wanted to, you could easily hand the sail and re-set it on the other gybe.

Handing is an equally controlled operation. The sheet and guy are both eased in order to spill some wind and reduce drive, then the bell is hauled down over the sail with its continuous line, easing the sheet and guy further as necessary. When the spinnaker has been completely swallowed by the Spee Squeezer or Sally, the sausage can be lowered onto the foredeck and the pole taken in and stowed.

Neither device will solve all spinnaker handling problems, but for the family crew or for those sailing singlehanded I think it is of very real value. Several competitors in the *Observer* Singlehanded Transatlantic Race have used it to good effect and, after a short acquaintance, I have been extremely impressed.

## Winching

The golden rule for winches should be that you *never* leave a handle in a winch if it can be removed. To help people remember to take the handle out, provide an easy stowage place for it near at hand. There are proprietary brands of plastic pockets on the market, but a handy locker is just as good, or a length of plastic tubing can be used at much less cost.

Never sit on a winch under load, never crouch astride a sheet to grind it in and never stand in the vee of a sheet where it passes through a turning (foot) block before going onto its winch. If there are no other seats or there is no other position from which you can apply your full strength without getting in the way of the person tailing, there is something very wrong with the cockpit layout and it should be changed.

Do make sure before working a sheet or halyard winch that you are in a comfortable and secure position. With a sheet winch you should be able to apply your full body weight to assist your arms before ever changing to a lower gear to grind in a headsail. Don't allow anyone to haul in the slack of a sheet ahead of the winch, it is the surest way I know to create a riding turn on the barrel. Rattle in the slack with just one or two turns round the barrel, then lay on at least two more turns and begin to grind in while someone else tails. If you have to do the tailing yourself, work the winch with whichever hand draws the handle across your chest, and tail with the other. This means you are using the stronger muscles on the inside of your forearm and can apply much more of your body weight. If you try to use the muscles down the outside of your forearm and push the handle away from your body, as though playing a backhand in tennis, you will find you have much less power.

When you want to ease a sheet by surging it round a winch, uncleat it and then use the heel of one hand pressed against the turns on the barrel to control the rate of release. Never use your fingers.

If you need to get all the turns off quickly, for instance when tacking, pull the tail vertically and, when they are clear, let go. Don't try to unwind the turns, the sheet will be dragged out through your hand if there is any weight of wind and, if it is not, then it will twist up and snarl in the fairlead.

A fairly recent development is the self-tailing winch which doesn't require either the person working the winch or a helper to keep the sheet under load as it comes off the barrel; a self-tailer does it all for you. The sheet is led off the top of the barrel, over a stripper and into a gripping wheel mounted on top of the winch. This wheel turns with the barrel and maintains a constant tension in the sheet, preventing any accidental slipping of the turns on the barrel and consequent slackening of the sheet.

Basic operations remain the same as for conventional winches during sail handling, but only one person is required to work the winch and, when a sheet is to be let fly, it is pulled out of the gripper and the turns are taken off the barrel by unwinding them to avoid the stripper. Care must be taken here not to trap your fingers when the turns slip as they are removed and it is probably safer to surge the sheet round the barrel, controlling it with the heel of your hand, so that wind is spilt from the sail and only when there is no strain on the sheet should the turns be unwound.

Undoubtedly these winches are a great boon to lightly crewed boats and in time they are likely to become more common than conventional types.

Where a halyard, usually the main, is fitted with a reel winch to hold the complete wire fall, great care must be exercised. Before hoisting, the turns on the barrel must be sorted out so that they don't overlap, and the slack must be wound on by holding the fall under tension above the winch with one hand and turning the winch handle with the other. Once the sail is hoisted, hold the handle firmly and screw down the winch

brake hard. Remove the handle and check that the brake is not slipping. When you want to get the mainsail down, unscrew the brake slowly and don't unscrew it completely, rather let it drag very slightly so that the sail has to be pulled down. This sounds daft, but if it is let go entirely the turns can spring open and jam. Whatever you do mind your fingers if you have to sort out the wire, whether under any load or not, because it is very easy to trap them.

CHAPTER SIX

# ANCHORING

On a dark, squally night with a rocky shore rather too close under your lee there is no insurance policy better than a big, heavy anchor well dug in at the end of a long chain cable. Even if you keep your boat in a marina and hope never to have to anchor beyond a brief stop for lunch, there is no excuse for carrying inadequate ground tackle or for stowing it in such a way that it is not readily available. The person who advocates stowing the anchor in a locker somewhere aft, or even down below, and advises that the rope cable can be kept in a locker under the sail bags should be sent to sea – he has clearly never been there and is a dangerous man.

## Anchor stowage

When considering anchor stowage it must be borne in mind that, although it may not be needed on a passage of several days duration, the anchor must be instantly ready to let go when entering port. There is no way of predicting when or for what reason you may suddenly require it, but there is no surer way of stopping the boat than anchoring, and having good ground tackle leaves you independent of moorings and marinas. To this end all lashings must be arranged to hold the anchor firmly in place but must be easily undone.

In recent years there has been a move away from stowing anchors in wooden chocks on the foredeck, and most new boat designs incorporate a well in which the anchor (and sometimes the cable) is stowed. A hatch covers the well leaving the foredeck clear of an otherwise large obstruction.

An alternative to deck stowage in the normal sense is to stow the anchor in the bow roller. This is generally done with a plough type anchor, and the roller is designed to fit the shape between shank and plough. On some boats the roller is at the stemhead and the shank lies aft along the deck, while on others a stub bowsprit is fitted to carry the roller further forward. With this arrangement the anchor is entirely forward of the stem and, when lying at anchor, the cable is held clear so that it cannot chafe against the stem.

Where the boat has a bowsprit and standing bobstay the plough of a plough type anchor can be hooked under the stay and the cable bowsed taut to hold it securely. Letting go then simply entails paying out cable.

Both of these arrangements allow the anchor to be dropped immediately, with the benefit of not having to pick up a heavy, clumsy object and try to pass it out through the pulpit. If a plough type anchor does have to be stowed on deck it is best laid with the bottom of the ploughshare parallel and close to the toerail. By doing so it is kept as near to the edge of the foredeck working area as possible.

Meon type anchors with their flat blades and long 'anti-roll' bars are less easily stowed anywhere other than on deck or in an anchor locker. They can be laid flat in deck chocks and are less of a nuisance there in some respects than a plough anchor where the blades stand up rather high, but it is often better to stand a meon up and lash it to the pulpit. This is normally done at one side so as to leave the bow roller clear and to keep the anchor away from the forestay. Before adopting this arrangement, make sure the headsails will not chafe too much on the stowed anchor.

Those are the two commonest yacht anchors today, but the fisherman is still used as a kedge. Most people fold the stock down against the shank and stow it in a locker somewhere, but it can well be lashed to the pushpit or laid in chocks on deck. For permanent readiness you can adopt the old practice of leaving the anchor set up and stowing it in chocks on the sidedeck by the shrouds, with the flukes laid close to the coachroof and the stock vertically down the topsides outside the rail.

A new type of anchor, the Bruce Anchor, developed for mooring offshore oil rigs, presents some stowage problems, as the blades and shank are one solid unit. The anchor can be kept in a stemhead or bowsprit fitting in the same way as a plough type anchor, or there are special chocks available for it. These however mean keeping the anchor right in the middle of the foredeck. One other solution is to hang the anchor under the forward rail of the pulpit.

## Preparing to let go

When an anchor cable is fed down the chain pipe into the locker below, it piles up in a cone then, when the boat is sailing and is heeled over, the cone collapses. If the cable is not used for a time it can get rather tangled up so, before trying to anchor, you should overhaul the chain by getting a few fathoms out on deck and running it back into the locker. This ensures that when you do let go, the cable will run out freely.

A rope cable must be flaked down on deck not coiled, else it will certainly snarl up when the anchor is let go. Another way of avoiding this problem is to stow the line on a reel that can be mounted on the foredeck and from which the cable can run out freely. When the anchor is recovered the line is wound back onto the reel and stowed away.

To make doubly certain the chain will run out without any hitches, some people like to range a few fathoms on deck in a series of fore and aft loops. The cable is turned up on the bitts and only the amount on deck can run out.

When the cable has been overhauled or ranged on deck, the anchor can either be laid with its shank in the bow roller and the plough or blades pointing out ahead, or it can be hung down over the stem with the shackle joining it to the cable right up against the bow roller. In either case there is then no need to lift the anchor about before dropping it: it is ready to go. The anchor can only be hung from the bow roller in calm water of course, or it will swing against the stem.

If there is any likelihood of there being obstructions on the bottom, such as old mooring ground chains, a tripping line and buoy are attached to a ring on the crown of the anchor. The buoy floats the line and, if the anchor fouls, the line can be hauled in to trip the anchor out by its crown thus pulling it out backwards. This will not always clear a fouled anchor, but it is a simple precaution worth taking. Keep an eye open for any idiots picking up your tripping line thinking it is a mooring buoy – it does happen.

## Letting go, veering and making fast

When the spot to anchor has been chosen (having regard to the proximity of other moored craft, the depth of water now and at low tide, the ease of approach and exit from the berth, etc), the helmsman must bring the boat up to it with only a little way on, so that the anchor is let go when either the boat is still carrying a little headway or has stopped and is making a little sternway. Which direction of movement is employed is up to you, but the boat must not be completely stationary when the anchor hits the bottom or the cable will pile up on top of it and foul it. I prefer to anchor when making sternway for, although it means overshooting the berth a little and dropping back into it, the cable is immediately carried clear of the stem and does not scrape along the topsides. If the boat is still going ahead when the anchor bottoms she will over-ride the cable and possibly damage the paintwork.

When the helmsman judges the boat to be in the right place he calls 'Let go', and the foredeck hand either drops the anchor so that the cable rattles out until the anchor hits the bottom when he checks it with a foot against the fairlead, or he lowers the anchor and cable with a controlled (but quick) hand-over-hand movement. If a winch is used, then the brake on this is used to slow and stop the cable as it runs out. Again it is up to you which method you use, but if you simply let go, do not do so until you are sure you are not standing in a bight of the cable

which could trap your feet. When you try to stop the cable wear shoes or boots and use your heel not your toes. Make sure also that the cable is made fast at its bitter end, or the whole lot could run out. If you choose to pay out the cable warn the helmsman, as he must take the slower bottoming of the anchor into account while deciding when to give the order to let go.

A tripping line is most easily set by throwing both buoy and line well clear of the boat immediately before dropping anchor. Ensure that the line is led out through the pulpit from the anchor and that it will run clear. Also of course, be sure the line is long enough to cope with the depth at high water.

As soon as the anchor is on the bottom pay out a couple of fathoms and take a turn on the bitts to snub the anchor in, making sure you keep your fingers well clear. Place a hand on the cable below the bow roller and feel if the anchor is still dragging by the vibration in the cable. If it is dragging, veer more scope until it stops. Once that has happened, you can safely veer the full scope required without fear of its piling up on the anchor and fouling it.

The usual maxim for the scope required, is three times the depth at high water for all-chain cable, and five times the depth at HW for chain and line. These however are absolute minima and, if the anchorage is going to get rough, the

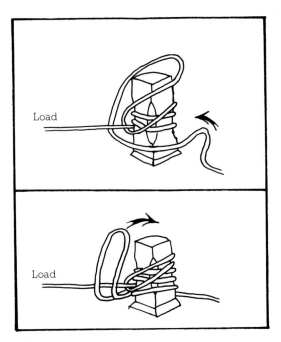

FIG. 4
Securing a line or anchor chain to a samson post.

the post. Another bight of the lazy end is taken and the process repeated passing the bight under the working part in the opposite direction. Never make fast with the load bearing part as the cable cannot then be undone while still under tension (which may be very great). If instead of a post there is a double-headed bollard, the cable is turned up in figures of eight around the two heads, and if there is a simple cleat it is made up in the usual way. Where there is a post with an athwartship bar through it (a staghorn) the cable can be made up in figures of eight or with the 'no-name' knot as used on a samson post. Again, *never* make up using the load bearing part of the cable.

When the anchor is down and the boat has settled back, take a series of visual bearings to check her position and, after you have had a cup of coffee or whatever, check them again to see that she's not dragging. A new set of bearings will be needed when the tide turns, but keep an eye on her position until she has lain there for at least one change of tide.

Rig a bow fender if one is available. This goes round the stem beneath the cable and stops damage to the topsides if the boat rides over the cable. Also remember with an anchor warp to fit anti-chafe gear at the fairlead if the weather is likely to turn nasty. This can best take the form of a length of heavy plastic tubing split lengthwise and slipped

figures can well be raised to five and seven respectively.

Once the required scope has been veered you can make the cable fast on the bitts. If there is a samson post, use the 'no-name' knot: the cable is passed round it a couple of times and a bight of the inboard part is passed under the load bearing part ahead of the post, brought up and dropped down over the head of over the warp, split uppermost, then lashed in position.

## Mooring and restricting swing

In an anchorage where the bottom offers uncertain holding or where shelter is rather poor, it is common practice to moor a cruiser by the head between two anchors. Besides providing more security this also restricts the swing of the boat on the change of tide, which is often desirable in a tight anchorage. Other ways of restricting a boat's swinging arc are mooring fore and aft, and mooring with two anchors in tandem.

To moor a boat by the head one anchor is let go and snubbed well in, then double the final scope is veered while the boat is moved across to where the second anchor will lie. This may be directly up or down tide or at right angles to an expected windshift. When the full scope is reached the second anchor is let go and the boat is centred between the two. The cable of the second anchor (usually a rope line on the kedge) is bent onto the cable of the bower anchor with a rolling hitch, and enough extra scope is veered to drop the hitch down below the bottom of the keel. Keep the rest of the kedge line on deck so that if anything happens to the rolling hitch the anchor is not lost. Now the boat is lying moored to the two anchors with

the cable of the bower anchor made up on the bitts.

If you are already lying to a single anchor and decide to lay out a second, you will either have to take the second anchor out and lay it from the dinghy, or move your boat under sail or power across to the spot where you want the second anchor, veering scope on the bower anchor as you go. With the second anchor set you centre up and bend the line to the bower cable and drop it down as before.

In a confined anchorage, such as a creek, where you wish to lie in a particular spot so as not to dry out at low water, you may decide to moor the boat fore and aft between two anchors; a flying moor. In this case you prepare the kedge on the after deck and, as you approach your intended berth, you drop the kedge and veer scope to twice the required length. Bring up hard on the kedge to snub it in and let go the bower anchor. Haul back on the kedge line veering cable on the bower, and centre the boat between the two anchors. Naturally, enough scope must be veered on both to allow for the rise and fall of tide, but don't overdo it or the boat will drift out of her allotted place at low water and may ground.

A boat's swinging arc may also be limited by dropping a kedge anchor under foot on a very short scope, so that

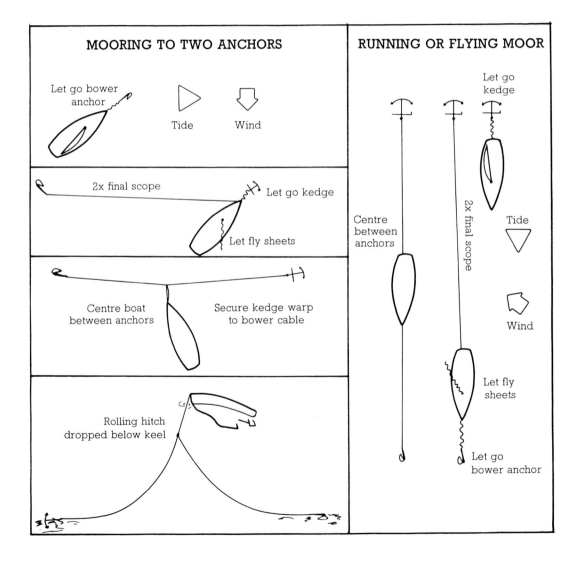

MOORING TO TWO ANCHORS

Let go bower anchor

Tide

Wind

2x final scope

Let go kedge

Let fly sheets

Centre boat between anchors

Secure kedge warp to bower cable

Rolling hitch dropped below keel

RUNNING OR FLYING MOOR

Let go kedge

Centre between anchors

2x final scope

Tide

Wind

Let fly sheets

Let go bower anchor

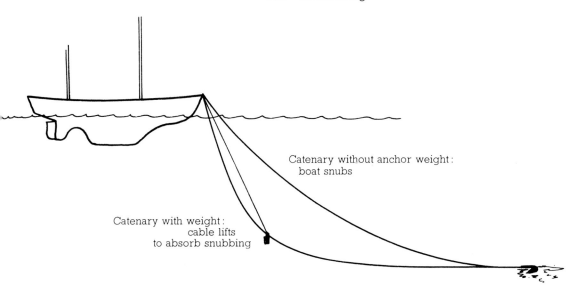

Catenary without anchor weight:
boat snubs

Catenary with weight:
cable lifts
to absorb snubbing

it just digs and drags on the bottom as the boat sheers and swings. An adaptation of this to add power to an anchor in a blow is to shackle a second anchor onto the bower cable a couple of fathoms back from the bower in tandem with it.

Another way of helping the anchor and reducing swinging arc when lying to a long scope is by using a cable weight. This is made up of a number of lead weights attached to a saddle which slides down the anchor cable (and can be retrieved by a line attached to it). The weight exaggerates the catenary of the cable, giving a lower angle of pull at the anchor and thus helping it to remain dug in. The weight also greatly reduces snubbing in very rough conditions, when otherwise the boat would raise her bows to an oncoming wave, be pushed astern, and bring up hard against the cable. With the weight on the cable the boat lifts the weight and straightens the cable

FIG. 5
Mooring to two anchors and the running or flying moor.

FIG. 6
The use of an anchor weight to lessen snubbing.

relatively gently. If no such weight is carried and the boat is snubbing, the strain on the cable can be eased by bending a nylon line onto it, about a fathom out from the bows, and transferring the strain to that. The nylon, being a stretchy material, will absorb the worst of the jerking, but keep the main cable made fast just in case the nylon parts. Anti-chafing gear should be fitted to the relieving line in the same way as for a normal rope anchor cable.

## Weighing anchor

Unless there is plenty of deep water all round or you are getting underway with the engine ticking over, it is usually necessary to cast the boat's head off in one particular direction. To allow this to be done the foredeck hand hauls in the anchor cable until it is straight up and down with the anchor right under foot, then calls or signals 'Up and down' to the helmsman. He and any sheet hands in the cockpit then back the headsail or do whatever is necessary to cast the boat's head round. As it comes round the order is given 'Break out' and the foredeck hand puts his back into it and breaks the anchor clear of the bottom, being sure to have one foot braced behind him so as not to be thrown off balance, and calls or signals 'Anchor's aweigh'. The helmsman is then free to start the boat moving. He must not sail her too fast else the remainder of the cable and the anchor itself will scrape over the hull as it is brought in.

When the anchor comes up to the bow roller it will often be covered in mud or have weed clinging to it, which will have to be cleaned off either with a brush or by dunking the anchor up and down in the water. Not until it is quite clean should it be brought aboard and stowed. Once the anchor is stowed and any mud and debris cleaned off the foredeck, the boat can be sailed at her normal pace.

A small boat in a rough sea can pitch so much that her bows practically go under and any foredeck work becomes dangerous, particularly weighing anchor as there is the constant chance of losing your footing or trapping your fingers in the cable. To sit down or crouch low is the safest plan and, if you need to stand to haul the cable, brace one foot behind you. When the bows are pitching make use of the fact. Haul in cable as they drop and snub it as they rise, that way you only haul in slack cable. It does need quick timing though to snub at the right moment, but *mind your fingers.*

It is fairly obvious that the larger the boat the heavier the ground tackle and so the harder it is to weigh anchor. On boats over about 40ft (say 12m) it may require more than one person to get the cable in unless the boat is equipped with an anchor windlass. This may be manually operated by working a big lever back and forth or it may, on sophisticated vessels, be electrically operated. The chain comes in over a gipsy specially shaped to fit the links of cable, and a stripper guides the cable into the chain pipe. Unfortunately windlasses take up a lot of space on deck and sails often snag on them. If it is possible an excellent idea is to include the windlass in the anchor

FIG. 7
*The pattern for sailing out an anchor. Cast the boat's head round and sail her off on a close reach to the full extent of the anchor cable, then snub and tack. Gather in slack cable as you can, then at the limit of the cable again snub and tack. Gather in more slack and snub the cable to break the anchor out as it comes up and down. Sail away slowly after anchor has broken out allowing the crew to get it aboard without damaging the topsides. Inset shows cable being snubbed on the samson post: use at least two turns and keep your fingers clear.*

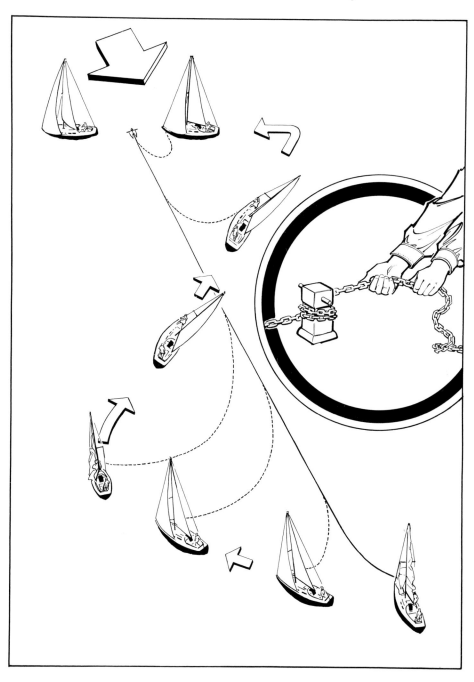

locker so that when the hatch is closed it
is beneath the deck.

Apart from breaking out the anchor,
perhaps the hardest part of weighing
anchor is getting that big hunk of metal
back through or over the pulpit. As you
struggle with it you will doubtless wish
for a self-stowing arrangement in the bow
roller or on a stub bowsprit, but while
you haven't got it, be very careful that the
plough or the meon blades don't trap and
crush your fingers – and don't drop the
anchor on your toes either.

## Sailing and motoring out an anchor

When an anchor has been really well
bedded in during a hard blow it may be
beyond the strength of the crew to break
it out by hand, and on such occasions you
must resort to sailing or motoring it out.

Taking motoring first as it is easier, put
the boat slow ahead while the crew
gathers in the slack cable. He must point
the direction in which the cable grows or
you will be motoring off at an angle
making his job harder instead of easier.
When the cable comes up and down he
must take a couple of turns on the bitts
*quickly*, keep his fingers clear, and snub
the anchor out as the boat passes over it.
You may have to open the throttle slightly,
but don't overdo it. Once he feels the
anchor has broken out, the foredeck hand

signals aft and the helmsman keeps the
boat in a straight line but throttles right
down. The rest of the cable is brought in
followed by the anchor, exactly as if it had
been brought in by hand.

Sailing out the anchor is slightly more
complicated and requires equally good
timing to snub the cable without trapping
your fingers. First get the boat underway
by backing the headsail to cast her head
round and letting draw as soon as
possible. Sail the boat close to the wind,
but not too close, you must keep her
moving fast. As she reaches the limit of
the cable, snub it, tack and begin to
gather in the slack, then as you reach the
limit in the opposite direction, snub and
tack again and keep on bringing in slack
cable. This or the next board should take
the boat close to or over the anchor, so as
soon as the cable comes roughly up and
down it must be snubbed so that the
boat's way breaks the anchor out. Once it
is broken out, the boat should be slowed
right down so that the rest of the cable
and the anchor can be recovered without
damaging the topsides by dragging it in
over them.

## Fouled anchor

However careful you are about choosing
your anchorages you will eventually get
a fouled anchor. If you have had the

foresight to attach a tripping line, you may be able to free it by hauling on this, but if not or it doesn't work you could be in for a long struggle.

The next best thing after a tripping line is a chain collar. To make this you need a length of chain such as might be found between a kedge and its warp. Lay the chain out flaking it back and forth over a length of about 3ft then bind the various parts together, using wire if possible, to make as stiff a length of chain as you can. Bend the chain round in a loop, pass it over the anchor cable outside the bow roller and fasten the two ends together. Attach a strong line that is longer than the depth of the water and let the chain collar fall down the anchor cable (which must be hove up bar taut). If the cable is all chain you will actually be able to hear the collar sliding down if it is a fairly quiet day, but in any case you'll feel it. When the collar reaches the anchor it will have to be juggled over the anchor shackle onto the shank (assuming of course that we are talking about a stockless anchor such as a plough type). Whether you can do this or not will depend on the stiffness of the collar and the nature of the obstruction on which the anchor is fouled, but assuming you manage it, run it right down the shank and then ease the anchor cable right off. Haul up on the line attached to the collar and try to lift the anchor clear by its crown.

When the anchor fouls on an old ground chain it may be possible to heave the chain up off the bottom and pass a line under it to hold it up while the anchor is dropped off. You'll be lucky if you manage and it is back-breaking work, but it's worth a try. In the same way, as a last resort you can try motoring round in a wide semi-circle in the hope of turning the anchor and being able to break it out from the opposite direction.

The ultimate solution to a fouled anchor, for instance when it is blowing up badly and you have got to clear the anchorage while it is still possible, is to slip the cable, buoy it and come back another day to try again. With this at the back of your mind you must always ensure that the bitter end of the cable is secured with a lashing that can be cut easily, not with a shackle that will corrode and be impossible to undo. Try to make the lashing long enough to come up through the chain pipe so that it can be cut from on deck rather than having to grovel round in the cable locker for it. Use a fairly strong line just in case all the cable is allowed to run out one day – you don't want to lose the lot because the lashing breaks.

At the time of writing, early experiments indicate that the new Bruce anchor can be very difficult to clear if fouled, and I understand that the makers are producing a special collar that acts in

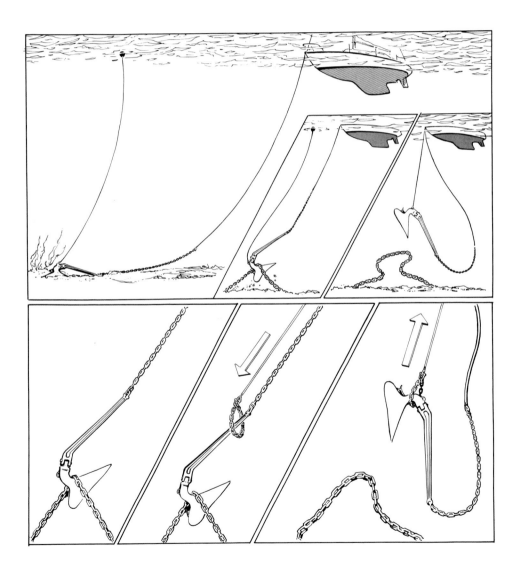

the same way as the chain one described above.

## Drudging

This is really controlled anchor dragging, as the anchor is broken out but left lying on the bottom and the boat is allowed to drift astern. The drag of the anchor means that the boat is moving slower than the current or tidal stream and water flows past the rudder. This being the case, the rudder can be used to steer the boat in a limited fashion and she can shift berth without recourse to either sails or engine.

Dragging the anchor over the bottom does rather invite fouling, but if a tripping line is used it can usually be avoided.

## Anchor and cable sizes

The following table is only a guide, but should suit most cruisers.

| LOA | Chain diameter | Rope diameter | Weight anchor plough/meon | Bruce |
|-----|-----|-----|-----|-----|
| ft | in | mm | lb | lb |
| 18 | 1/4 | 10 | 15 | 11 |
| 20 | 1/4 | 12 | 20 | 11 |
| 25 | 5/16 | 14 | 25 | 22 |
| 30 | 5/16 | 16 | 30 | 22 |
| 35 | 3/8 | 18 | 35 | 22* |
| 40 | 3/8 | 18 | 40 | 44 |

* This anchor is a little small for a 35-footer, but the next size up, the 44 lb is rather large and may present handling and stowage problems.

FIG. 8
Clearing a fouled anchor with the help of a tripping line and a chain collar. If you had the foresight to lay a tripping line as shown in the upper drawings, it may be possible to clear an anchor fouled (for example) on a ground chain by slackening off the cable and picking the anchor up by the tripping line attached to its crown. If you anchored without a tripping line you can try the chain collar method of recovery. In this case a ring of chain attached to a light line is run down the taut cable and onto the shank of the anchor. The cable is then eased away and the anchor lifted by its crown.

# CHAPTER SEVEN

# MOORING AND BERTHING

When coming in to pick up a mooring or to berth alongside, the crew must be given sufficient time to prepare boathooks, lines and fenders. They must be told on which side the fenders will be needed, what kind of mooring is to be picked up and what approach is to be made. A dummy run can be useful to everyone (skipper included) to make sure the plan is complete and that there is an escape route should anything go amiss. Once the berth or mooring has been selected and the crew given their instructions, it is aggravating to be told at the last minute that after all the lines and fenders will be needed on the other side. The ensuing scramble to shift them screams of poor seamanship and planning to everyone watching, and can well mean a snarl up of mooring lines, or fenders at the wrong height and in the wrong place.

On all occasions it must be made clear to the foredeck crew that, if he feels things are going wrong, he must inform the helmsman so that the pick up or berthing can be aborted and a fresh approach made. Equally if the helmsman is not happy he must say so and use his escape route to bring the boat round again.

## Single and double buoys

Unless the mooring to be picked up is

your home one or a familiar one, a dry
run is worthwhile to check what kind of
buoy or buoys you are dealing with. For a
start is it a single buoy which will be
brought aboard, one which will be left in
the water and the boat attached by a line
(is the line provided or will you have to
put one on?), or are there fore and aft
buoys that you will lie between?

If it is a buoy to be picked up and
brought aboard, is there a pick-up loop
on top that you can get a boathook into or
would it be easier to reach down with
your hand? Will you have to fish about
under water for the riser? If the buoy is to
be left in the water and a bridle for
securing the boat is provided, is there a
pick-up buoy on it or will you have to
pick up the line itself?

Where fore and aft buoys are used,
have they been left tied together and, if
so, which one will have to be made fast
forward and which will have to be
separated and led aft?

These are not the only variations that
can be found, but they should serve to
show that it is unwise simply to point to a
buoy lying astern of another boat of
about your size and say, 'We'll have that
one', then charge in full tilt and expect
your crew to get it. One important point
with an unfamiliar mooring is the question
of whether or not it is strong enough to
take your boat. Generally speaking, if you
pick up a buoy amongst boats of a similar
size to your own, you will be all right, but
if you are in any doubt check with
someone as soon as possible. In any case
it is best to find out if the owner of the
mooring is expected to return before you
plan to leave.

Should the owner return when you are
on his mooring it is of course good
manners to leave immediately and
without fuss. Few people will object to
your using their vacant mooring, but they
have every right to get angry if you
either refuse to move or have gone
ashore and left the boat unattended
without any indication of when you will
be back.

Once the proposed mooring has been
examined and the approach planned, the
helmsman brings the boat in on the
allotted heading while the foredeck crew
prepares to pick up the buoy. As it comes
under the bows it is likely that the
helmsman will lose sight of it, so the crew
must point to the buoy either with his arm
or the boathook, and if necessary he must
indicate how far there is left to go. This
can either be done verbally or by holding
up a number of fingers according to how
far away the mooring still is.

When the buoy comes within reach it
should be hooked up smartly, the
helmsman informed if he can't see, and
the mooring brought aboard. The
boathook is then either handed to a
second crewman or laid down on the

deck so that it can't roll overboard. The riser is hauled in under the pulpit and secured on the bitts. Finally all the spare line is coiled down tidily and if necessary the deck washed off.

Where there is a pick-up line attached to a buoy that remains in the water, there is likely to be a permanent loop in the end of the bridle and this can just be dropped over the mooring post or cleat. If on the other hand you have to attach a line to the buoy, prepare it by securing one end to the mooring bitts and leading the other out through the bow fairlead. As the buoy comes within reach, either one crewman hooks on and holds the buoy close while another passes the line through the ring in the top of the buoy, or you have to lie down, reach out and thread the line through and bring it back aboard before the boat's head falls off and the buoy goes out of reach.

An easier method of attaching a line to the buoy is to use a device called the Star Grabbit Boathook. This consists of a large hook with a spring-closed bar across its mouth and a strong line attached to one end. The line is made fast on the mooring bitts and the hook is loaded onto a track screwed to a pole (such as the back of an ordinary boathook) so that the spring bar is held open. The line is taken in one hand, the pole or boathook in the other and the buoy is hooked in the usual manner. The boathook is tugged to

release the hook which snaps shut and, hey presto, you are attached to the buoy. This device is particularly useful if you are picking up singlehanded as the line can be led from the bitts, out through the fairlead and aft outside all to the cockpit. You then make the pick up from the cockpit, saving a mad dash forward at the last moment. Be careful however that the line is not so long that you drop astern on it and hit the next boat.

If you are going to lie to a buoy where you have had to provide your own line and the weather is bad, some sort of chafing gear will be needed to prevent the line being worn through at the ring on the buoy. A length of plastic piping is good for this, but it will have to be lashed in place or the surging of the boat will work it out of position. A permanent bridle will probably have its own chafing gear fitted.

When picking up fore and aft double moorings they must be brought up and, if possible, the bow one made fast before separating them. This is not always possible though and you have to hold them against the pull of the boat while they are separated. Clearly two people make this easier. One holds the two buoys while the other unties them and then, while he takes the stern line aft, the first person turns up the bow mooring.

## Pile moorings

In some congested rivers boats lie moored between piles driven into the riverbed. Their bow and stern lines are secured to rings that slide up and down the piles so that no allowance has to be made for the rise and fall of tide; they are self-tending.

Securing between piles is usually much easier if another boat is already moored there, as you can just lie alongside and hold on while you run lines out to the piles. If the berth is empty the boat must be carefully positioned so that a bow or stern line can be secured, then moved ahead or astern so that the other line can be put on. This can be done under power but some pile moorings have a line permanently rigged between them to help. The crew holds on to the line and hauls the boat ahead or astern as necessary.

When the berth is occupied you must come alongside the next boat with the appropriate lines and fenders rigged (as will be described in a later section of this chapter) and make fast to her. Once that is done the dinghy can be used to run bow and stern lines to the piles.

Although it is not always done, it is wise when lying alongside another yacht to do so in a bow-to-stern manner so that as the boats roll together on washes, the masts will not foul each other.

## Boathook or hand?

Whether you use a boathook or your bare hand to pick up a mooring depends to a large extent on the freeboard at the bows (assuming that is where you will pick up from). On a boat with higher freeboard at the bows than the length of your arm, you have no option but to use a boathook. However, on smaller craft it is occasionally better to use your hand. Obviously this must be done with some caution if you are not to injure yourself, but the human hand provides a far more positive grip on a buoy than the best boathook.

The other reason for using your hand is that the mooring can be let go more readily if the pickup is to be aborted. Whether this is because the tide is too strong to hold the boat against or the boat is moving too fast, all you have to do to release the buoy is open your hand, whereas with a boathook you have to reach out even further to unhook it.

Arguing the other way, a boathook gives you a far longer reach than your arm and it can turn a miss into a successful pick up. In the end, as usual, it's up to you to use your judgement in the situation.

## Communications

Good communication between cockpit
and foredeck is essential if mooring
operations are to go smoothly. On most
boats this can be achieved verbally, but
if the motor is running it will mean
shouting and then words can be mistaken,
tempers lost and much embarrassment
felt when it is noticed how many people
are watching and listening.

For quieter communication an
established set of signals is required. I
have already mentioned that the person
actually carrying out the mooring pick-up
can signal the direction of the mooring by
pointing and holding up a number of
fingers to show distance in feet, yards or
metres (what the distance will be given in
must be decided beforehand).
Alternatively he can use signals such as
those shown below, but whatever is done
make sure that the person you are
signalling to will understand.
Turn to starboard–right arm outstretched
Hard a-starboard–wave arm to right
(pointing)
Turn to port–left arm outstretched
Hard a-port–wave arm to left (pointing)
As you go (ie straight ahead)–arm held
straight up
Come ahead–wave arm forward over
head
Full ahead–wave both arms
Go astern–wave arm over head facing aft

Full astern–use both arms
Slow down–wave slowly palm
downwards
Speed up–wave clenched fist quickly up
and down
Stop engine–arms crossed over head

## Making fast

The simplest mooring to secure to is a
single buoy that remains in the water and
has an attached bridle–all you have to do
is bring the bridle aboard and drop the
eye in its end over the bitts. Other types
require more skill than this however.

Where the buoy is to remain in the
water but a line has to be secured to the
ring on top, one end of the line to be used
is made up on the bitts, using the lazy end
not the part that will go to the buoy. If the
lazy end is used it can be undone under
load; if the working part were used it
could come under such strain as to be
impossible to slip. The working end is
then passed through the ring on the buoy
and brought back to the foredeck where
it is also turned up on the bitts. You may
have to make it up on top of the turns of
the other end, but that is to be preferred
to using a smaller, weaker cleat. Finally
some chafing gear should be put on.

A small buoy that is brought aboard
will usually be attached to a line or light
chain riser, which in turn is fastened to

the mooring chain. The line or chain is hauled aboard, and the mooring chain made fast just like an anchor chain with a 'no-name-knot' (see page 108). Where a large cleat is used the chain must be turned up in figures of eight; the same for twin-headed bollards. If a large bar (staghorn) is fitted through the head of the samson post some people use it like a cleat to hold figure of eight turns of the chain in preference to the 'no-name-knot'.

Always make fast using the lazy end of any line or chain – *never* use the working end (load bearing part).

## Leaving Moorings

When leaving a mooring under sail it will be necessary to cast the boat's head off in a particular direction, and this can usually be achieved by walking the mooring a short way aft on one side so that the current, stream or wind turns the boat. A small boat can be turned end for end like this by holding the mooring in one hand and walking aft, passing the buoy from hand to hand outside the shrouds, but if a larger boat is to be turned round it is better to use a bridle. This is done by securing a line to the buoy from the stern and another from the bow. The bow line is eased, the buoy dropped over into the water and the stern line hauled in. By checking away on the bow line and

heaving in on the stern one, the buoy is brought aft and the current, stream or wind again turns the boat.

This method requires that the lines can be slipped instantly otherwise the boat will be sailing away still attached to the buoy. The best way of doing this is to thread the line through the eyesplice beneath the buoy and have both ends on board. Then when you want to slip you throw one end clear and haul on the other, but make sure the line really is clear or else it will twist round the other and may jam.

When the helmsman gives the order to let go, throw the buoy and as much of the rope or chain as you can well clear of the boat so that, as it sinks, it will not foul the keel. Call out 'All gone' when it has.

Getting underway from a mooring using the engine is often easier than sailing off, but there is always the risk of fouling the propeller on the mooring. It is essential to throw the buoy and its riser well clear and then, as the engine is put into gear, to watch the buoy. If it shows any inclination to go under the hull the helmsman must be warned and the engine taken out of gear. Usually it is possible to go astern away from the mooring before going ahead, but not always and it is then that such care and attention pays off.

Before leaving fore and aft moorings the two buoys must be tied together, and for a short while the boat will have to hang off one mooring. Getting clear of this type of mooring can be tricky, particularly if rope risers are used as they float when dropped in the water. Think and plan carefully before letting go then throw the buoys well away.

Once clear of the mooring the deck can be washed off if necessary and any lines that were used coiled and returned to their stowage. If the boat was lying to a chain bridle and you used a bow fender, that too should be brought in – it's unseamanlike to sail with any fenders out unless you are about to berth.

## Berthing alongside

Whether it is intended to lie alongside another boat, a harbour wall or a marina pontoon the helmsman must study wind, tide and current while the crew prepares fenders and warps on the allotted side. If the proposed berth is alongside a rough staging or wall with a pile structure, a plank should be slung horizontally between the fenders and the wall to span a couple of the piles. If this is not done the fenders will roll off the piles and the boat's topsides will be damaged. Tying the fenders in pairs and using them horizontally (one above the other) is the next best thing if a plank is not available, but a frequent check must be made to see

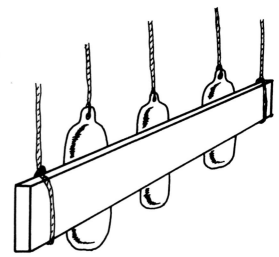

FIG. 9
A plank should be slung between the fenders and pilings when lying alongside a rough wall or pier...

that they do not slip off the piles.

For other berths the fenders should be spread out regularly along the vessel's side with their lines hitched (round turn and two half hitches normally) onto either the guardrail stanchion or a grabrail on the coachroof. It is better to use the stanchions as it leaves the sidedecks clear. Adjust the height of the fenders according to the height of whatever you are going to lie alongside; low down for a pontoon and about mid-height for another boat. Fine adjustments can be made after the boat has berthed.

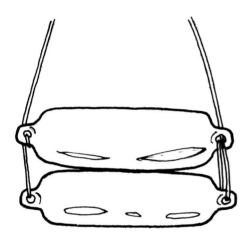

FIG. 10
...but when a plank is not available two fenders may be used together.

The stern line and head rope are the two mooring lines prepared first as they are the two sent across first. Bring the others on deck, but don't bother to set them up yet, they will only be in the way.

One end of the stern line is led over the guardrail and down under the pushpit where it is taken through a fairlead and turned up on the quarter cleat using the short lazy end, not the long working part. The line is then coiled *towards* the working end (so that it does not kink) and is led forward outside everything to the foredeck. It's taken up there so that someone can step ashore with it from just forward of the shrouds rather than having to wait until the stern is brought alongside; indeed the stern line must be put ashore early as it is usually required to slow the boat and help bring the stern in.

The head rope is dealt with similarly. The end is passed over the guardrail and dipped under the pulpit, where it is led through a fairlead and turned up on the bitts – again using the short lazy end and not the long working (load bearing end). The line is then coiled towards the working end and laid down ready for use.

During the preliminary look at the berth, one of the things to check is what the boat will be moored to. If there are rings in a wall or cleats on the deck of a boat or pontoon then there is no problem, but if there are dockside bollards the mooring lines will have to have bowlines put in their working ends to save time ashore. With this done they can simply be dropped over the bollards after the eye has been dipped up through the loops of any other lines there. It is important to dip your lines under any others so that the others can be released without disturbing yours.

On very large craft with heavy mooring lines, it may be necessary to send a heaving line ashore to haul the mooring warps across. If this is the case they

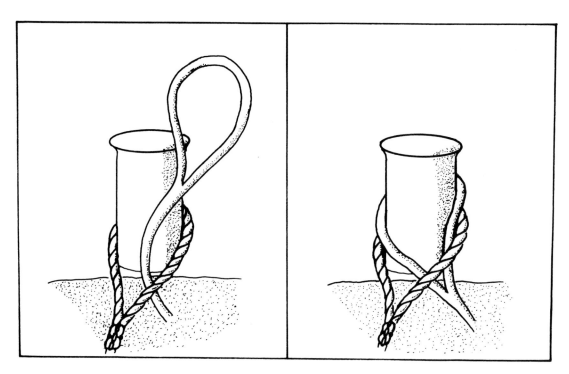

FIG. 11
The loop in the end of a mooring line should always
be dipped up through any existing lines before
being dropped over a bollard, as the other lines can
then be removed without yours being disturbed.

FIG. 12
Monkey's fist and heaving line bend.

should be bent onto the warps with heaving line bends and coiled down in two coils ready for throwing. A heaving line consists of a light line with a large weighted knot in one end (commonly a Monkey's Fist) and the other end is bent onto the warp by forming an eye in the warp and racking the end of the heaving line in and out across this eye. When thrown the heaving line is divided into two coils, one small and held in the throwing hand, the other large and held loosely in the other hand. The small coils are swung back and thrown hard with a sideways swinging motion similar to that used when throwing a discus. The large coils are allowed to run out freely. When the person ashore has caught the line he hauls the warp across.

While all the preparations on deck have been going on, the helmsman should have worked out his approach allowing for all outside influences. The prime objective must be to bring the boat alongside slowly and for the crew to put lines ashore quickly. If you have a choice of berths to lie in, select one where the wind and any current or tide will work to help rather than hinder, but be prepared to have to accept one that is less auspicious.

Where the wind is opposed to a current or tidal stream and you are going to berth under power (which is really the only sensible thing to do if your motor is working), choose if you can to head into the current or stream and let it slow you thus keeping your astern gear in reserve for final stopping and swinging the stern in.

If wind and current are in the same direction (or there is no current) you will of course come in head to wind if you can. Again astern gear can be used to slew the stern in.

Where the wind is blowing into the berth try to edge in at an angle, turning the ship's head out from the berth at the last moment and allow the wind to push her in.

With the wind out of the berth you may have to get lines ashore and warp the boat in the last few feet as she will tend to blow off.

As the yacht is brought in towards her chosen berth one of the crew takes up the stern line and positions himself on the sidedeck just forward of the shrouds ready to step ashore with it. Be careful not to jump too soon and go in the water, but get the line ashore as early as possible. If there are bollards on the quay or pontoon he should drop a loop over one of these (remembering to dip the eye up through any other lines already on the bollard) and leave another member of the crew to adjust the line from on board. With rings or cleats (for example on another yacht) he should make the line fast and again leave the adjustment to

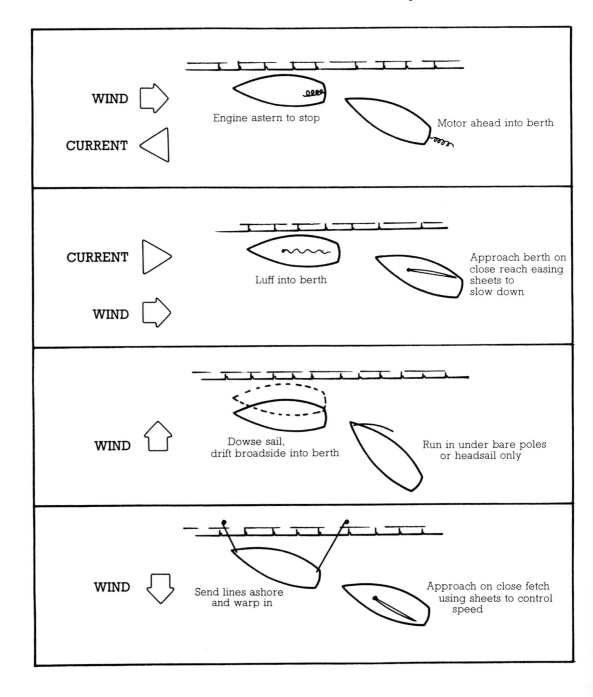

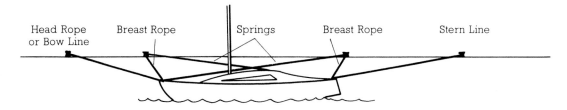

| Head Rope or Bow Line | Breast Rope | Springs | Breast Rope | Stern Line |

FIG. 14
Mooring lines.

someone on board. Once he has made up the stern line he runs forward and catches the bow line as it is thrown (passed) to him and secures that in the same way as the stern line. It is most important that the person on shore should not attempt to control the boat but leave it to the crew on board.

The conventional advice, as given above, is to send the stern line ashore first followed by the head rope, but an alternative when the approach is well controlled, is to run a line from a cleat amidships on the sidedeck down to the pontoon or quay. By holding this line taut the boat is kept from slewing across the dock, although her bow or stern may swing out a little, and she is provided with a good temporary mooring, though if staying for any length of time the normal mooring lines must be set up.

Any spare crew members must be deployed to fend off from the quay or boat that you are coming alongside and

to slow the yacht by surging the bow and stern lines round cleats, eventually making them fast when the boat is in the right position. If you have sufficient fenders it is worth leaving a spare one on deck so that it can be brought into use wherever it is needed. Fend off sensibly, don't do things like putting your foot against another yacht's stanchions if you are coming in too quickly, or step outside the guardrails to push against the quay.

Try to keep the stern line and head rope as long as possible, about the same length as each other, and adjust them so that the boat lies parallel to whatever you are lying alongside. If you come in next to another boat you must still put bow and stern lines ashore, don't risk securing to the boat alone and so putting the weight of both vessels on his shore lines or if it comes on to blow you could be in trouble.

Fore and aft springs should now be put out, the forward one running from the

FIG. 13
Plans for berthing alongside.

foredeck to a point on the quay (or next boat) level with the stern of your own boat, and the after spring should go from the quarter to somewhere near the bows. If you are alongside another yacht the springs should be made fast to her. Springs hold the boat close into her berth and stop her moving fore and aft. Breast ropes can be put out if required, but they are not often needed.

Some slack must be left in mooring lines to allow for the rise and fall of tide. Until you know how much will be needed someone must stay aboard to make the adjustment, but once the boat has been tended through a complete tidal cycle it is usually possible to leave her. In areas of very great tidal range someone might have to stay on board all the time, because if the lines are too slack at high water the boat will surge around and could be damaged. Heavy weights suspended from the lines will help to take up slack at high water but they may not solve the problem.

As we explained earlier, when planning to lie alongside another yacht try to do so with your bows to her stern. Remember also to go ashore across her foredeck, never across her cockpit, and if there is anyone on deck it is courteous to ask permission to cross. Walk quietly, particularly at night and try not to leave a trail of mud, sand or grit across the decks.

If someone wants to come alongside you, let them, take their lines, and should you not want them there for some reason, argue the toss after they are secured. Don't start shouting and waving at them as they approach, they have got enough on their minds already. Try to sort yourselves out so that smaller boats lie outside larger ones, everyone will be more comfortable that way.

If you are in a marina and are not lying in a visitor's berth you must of course be prepared to move out when the owner returns. Check with the berthing master to see if he is expected back before you plan to leave.

### Drying out alongside

After you have secured alongside in a drying harbour go ashore and check with the local authorities that the bottom is fairly flat. If it is not you may have to move.

Assuming the bottom is reasonable, the most important thing is to make sure the yacht will not fall outwards from the wall as the tide drops. Initially the boat is heeled inwards by shifting weight to the side next to the wall; the anchor and chain ranged along the sidedeck is the usual method. For added security a line must be taken ashore from the mast, either a halyard (which can be adjusted from on deck) or a warp from the hounds.

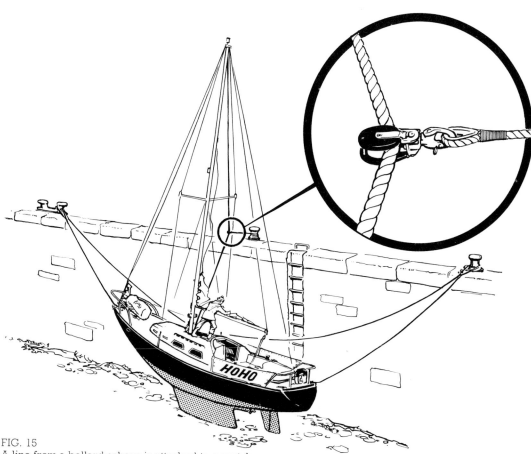

FIG. 15
A line from a bollard ashore is attached to a snatch
block running on a taut halyard to hold the boat well
in as she dries out alongside. Once the correct
length of the mooring lines has been set, this system
makes the boat self-tending throughout each tidal
cycle.

In either case the line will have to be taken up as the tide falls and then eased as it rises again. It may be possible to use a heavy weight suspended from the line to do this, but keep an eye on it for at least one tide. A self-tending set up is successfully achieved by taking a line ashore from a snatch block running up a taut halyard. Remember too that the dinghy painter will need to be lengthened as the tide falls.

When the yacht is dried out, unless she has a full length flat keel, move fore and aft cautiously, or at any rate don't let all the crew dance on the foredeck at once.

While bilge keelers do not need heeling in towards the wall when drying out, it is particularly important to choose an almost flat bottom to sit on. If it slopes away steeply from the wall, the boat *could* heel out and fall over. It has to be pretty bad for that to happen, but take care.

## Berthing stern-to

It is the custom in many harbours to berth stern-to the quay rather than alongside it. This makes getting ashore easier as you do not have to clamber over all the boats lying inside you, but it calls for skilful boat handling when there is a cross wind blowing.

The usual procedure is to lay an anchor out from the quay or pick up a buoy there and then move stern first into a slot at the quay. You then put two stern lines ashore, fenders out on both sides and perhaps springs onto the next door boats.

With a cross wind this operation can be difficult, as the boat's stern will try to turn up into the wind as you go in. Careful snubbing of the anchor cable can help straighten her up again, but the crew may also have to do some quick work with fenders and lines. Another plan is to anchor, send a line ashore in the dinghy and haul in on that, but care must be taken not to land athwart the bows of the next boat.

As most boats have better control when going ahead than when going astern it may be easier to berth bows on rather than stern to. If you do this you must pick the buoy up from the cockpit or lay out an anchor from there. Getting ashore over the bows is not quite so easy as from the stern, but at least no one on the quay can stand and stare into the cabin.

When there is a cross wind blowing, all the boats at the quay will be lying down wind from their anchors, so try to lay yours slightly up wind from your final berth.

## Leaving an alongside berth

First of all if you have to leave and there is an unattended boat outside you, it is your responsibility to moor her safely in your berth. You will have to cast off her springs and bring in one of her shore lines, and you must leave someone to re-moor her after you have moved out.

Assuming you are in an outside berth whether alongside a quay wall or another boat, study the wind and current or tidal stream before doing anything. If the wind is blowing you out of the berth and there is a current from ahead, you are in a nice position as the bows may be canted out a little, the helm put over and the wind and tide will see you clear. It is when all the forces are holding you in the berth that the fun starts.

Whether you decide to leave bow or stern first will depend on individual circumstances; width of the channel, direction of the harbour entrance, surrounding craft. Under the right circumstances there is no reason why you should not leave under sail, but make sure there is room. In a very tight berth such as a marina, it is sometimes convenient to warp the boat out rather than try to turn her under power. Circumstances will dictate.

One useful way of getting the boat's head or stern well clear of the quay is by using the springs. For example if you remove all other lines and leave just the forward spring (from bow to shore near the stern) you have only to put the helm over a bit, go ahead on the engine and the boat's stern will swing out. A fender will be needed to protect the bows and if you do the reverse using the after spring to get her bows out, you will need a fender on the quarter. Once the bow or stern has started to swing, ease back on the throttle, middle the helm and take the boat out, slipping the spring as you go.

To facilitate slipping and recovery of such lines as the springs, prepare to leave your berth by bringing both ends of the line aboard; one end can then be let go and the line recovered by hauling on the other end. If the line runs through a ring in a harbour wall, let go the *lower* end so that it hangs clear of the ring and can be pulled through easily. If the top part is let go it can jam as the lower part is hauled on.

When the skipper has decided how the boat will be taken out of her berth, the crew usually pulls in the bow and stern lines and breast ropes then doubles the springs so that both ends are on board. Do remember if the boat dried out to bring in the line from mast to quay. Try to keep all mooring lines out of the water, which is often oily, and coil them up neatly as soon as possible. Many mooring warps will be too big to coil in your hands, and must be coiled down on the deck then secured by lengths of line at say three points around the coil to keep them neat when stowed away. Lighter lines are coiled and secured using a buntline hitch.

On the command to slip the remaining lines throw one end clear and haul in smartly on the other, making sure they are clear of the propeller and trailing them in the water as little as possible. From alongside a pontoon or another yacht there is no reason why the lines should go in the water at all. As the boat clears her berth bring in the fenders and clean them if necessary before stowing them. Leaving fenders dangling and warps trailing is both unsightly and unseamanlike, so tidy up quickly.

Getting away from an alongside berth between piles may involve using the dinghy to free the lines, but otherwise there is little difference. If the sliding rings with the lines attached are under water, haul them to the surface and undo them from there, don't try to reach down into the water.

Leaving a stern to berth means slipping the springs and two stern lines then either hauling off to the anchor or buoy and getting underway from there, or you can motor slowly out, pick up the anchor (drop the buoy) and go straight out. If you berthed bows on the process should be the same.

# CHAPTER EIGHT

# DINGHIES ON DECK

The best place for any dinghy at sea is on deck. It takes up a lot of space, can obstruct forward vision and creates windage, but anything is better than towing.

The great advantage of an inflatable for small cruisers is the fact that it can be deflated and stowed either on the coachroof under the boom or in a locker, usually one of the cockpit lockers. If it is stowed on the coachroof there may be room to carry it with only the bow or stern section deflated and the other still pumped up. In an emergency the dinghy can be launched and will support the crew until they can complete its inflation. A half inflated dinghy is also very useful for recovering a person from the water. For short distances, an inflatable may be towed with its bow lashed up to the pushpit, and only its stern in the water, but even like this it can be flipped over by a strong wind or squall.

It requires a rather larger yacht to be able to carry a reasonable size rigid tender on the coachroof, but again this is the best place for it. The main question is which way up should it be carried? If it is carried the right way up it will collect rain and spray, needing frequent bailing or a fitted cover, but it is useful for stowing sail bags, warps and fenders in and it offers a useful handhold while working on deck. When stowed upside down the dinghy will not collect water, but it can't be used very well for stowage. Small things can be tucked under it but that is all. There should also be hand rails (doubling as runners) fitted along the dinghy's bilges so that you can hold on when going forward, as the coachroof grabrails will probably be covered up.

Various collapsible dinghies have come and gone over the years. They are still a good idea as they are easier to stow than a rigid dinghy and are easier to row than an inflatable, but there are few on the market.

The only other alternative to towing the dinghy is to sling it in davits on the stern. These look like a pair of miniature cranes mounted on the after deck. Wires are hooked onto strong points in the dinghy and it is winched up to lie under the arms of the davits clear of the water. It must be winched up very hard and is best lashed in tightly with extra lines as it always seems to swing about a little when there is a sea running. There is also the possibility of the dinghy being swamped by a wave when the boat is hard pressed and that can put great strain on all the davits' gear.

Any dinghy that is carried on deck must be well secured. Specially shaped chocks to fit snugly round the gunwales or bilges (depending on which way up she is carried) are a good start. Eyebolts in the deck for lashing down are also required. These must be through bolted to back-up pads as they can take a great strain in rough weather when green seas may attack the dinghy, or the boat may simply be thrown about a lot and the dinghy try to shift.

Some people make up webbing straps that go over the dinghy and are fastened with quick release fittings, but these must be made so that they can be tightened properly. If simple rope lashings are used, pass lines over and diagonally across the dinghy then tension them by bowsing them together with horizontal lines. Finish the lashings off with knots (round turn and two half hitches) that can be undone quickly. It is a good thing too to let all the crew know how the dinghy has been lashed down so that any of them can unfasten it in the dark.

## Launching and recovering dinghies

An inflatable that has been stowed deflated must of course be pumped up before it is launched and on a small boat this is not too easy because of the lack of any large flat deck area. Normally it is easier to pump the dinghy up on the foredeck, with the bow and stern laid across the guardrails than to try to do it in the cockpit. The pump can be worked by foot on the foredeck to inflate one side and if the second inflation point is on the opposite side it can be reached from a position by the mast.

With the inflated dinghy already laid across the guardrails and the painter made fast there is little difficulty even for one person to launch it over the side and into the water.

Recovering an inflatable aboard similarly presents little difficulty. The painter is used to pull the bows up to the rail and then, with one person on each side, the whole dinghy can be lifted aboard and lashed down, or if it is to be deflated it can be laid across the foredeck or cabin top. Deflation can then be carried out by opening the valves and leaving it to exhaust most of the air naturally before attempting to fold and roll the dinghy to force the remaining air out, or it can be forced out from the start, but surprisingly little time is saved if this is attempted. Once deflated the dinghy can be bagged up and stowed, or if only one section (usually the stern) was deflated it can be lashed down on the coachroof.

Rigid dinghies are rather harder work, for although a very small pram dinghy can be brought aboard by two people in the same way as an inflatable, most rigid tenders require the use of some lifting gear.

When the dinghy is small enough to bring aboard by hand it is more easily achieved if the guardrails are dropped to the deck. By doing that the dinghy need only be lifted to the height of the toerail (which needs protection with a rubbing strip of brass) and hauled aboard. It is then either turned and set down on the coachroof or capsized into its chocks and lashed in place.

The main halyard and its winch are normally sufficient lifting gear to bring a tender on board, but some very heavy dinghies may require the use of a derrick. This may take the form of a spinnaker pole swung outboard on the main halyard with a tackle at its outboard end which is used to lift the dinghy, or perhaps even the boom and mainsheet could be used. The painter is used as a guy to hold the derrick in place fore and aft during lifting. Once raised the dinghy can be swung inboard.

To bring the dinghy aboard with the main halyard, the painter is first brought in over the dinghy's bows and fastened at the stern. A loop is made in the painter at about the dinghy's point of fore and aft balance using a figure of eight knot. The halyard is then clipped into this and the dinghy is swayed up. The winch will probably have to be used and someone will be needed to keep the dinghy clear of the ship's side, bring her inboard and help capsize her on the cabin top.

Launching is really the reverse of recovering from the water. First the dinghy must be turned the right way up, then the halyard or lifting tackle is attached and the dinghy is lifted and lowered into the water.

When launching or recovering any dinghy, keep the painter or some other line from the dinghy made up on the parent vessel.

# CHAPTER NINE

# GOING ALOFT

There are any number of reasons for going aloft, from reeving off a new halyard to conning the ship through coral. Whatever the reason you can be pretty sure that one day you will have to go aloft and it is much easier to try out methods at anchor on a quiet day than it is to experiment at sea when the boat is rolling around.

Just as there are many reasons for going aloft so too are there many ways of getting there. The most common of these are discussed below, but it should be mentioned that despite having a mast stepped in a tabernacle, you can't feel smug and ignore this problem. It is an easy job to lower a mast in harbour, but at sea it is simply not on and you must therefore use the same systems as anyone else.

### Bosun's chair

This is the traditional way of going aloft. The chair is shackled onto a halyard and the man in it is hauled up. Modern bosun's chairs are made of canvas and are worn rather like a pair of nappies (diapers). A webbing suspension strap has a steel ring at its apex and the halyard is shackled onto this. Pockets are usually provided for carrying tools in. More conventional chairs are a simple wooden board with rope used to form a sling for hoisting. An eye is seized in the apex of the sling and the halyard shackled to it.

Both types have their advantages and disadvantages: while the modern canvas chair is strapped together so that the occupant can't fall out, it tends to clamp the thighs tightly together, making hanging onto the mast difficult while also cutting off the circulation in your legs if you have to be aloft for any length of time. The board type of chair needs a lashing round the person's waist to hold him in, but there is plenty of room to grip the mast between your thighs and, very importantly in rough seas when he may be swung violently against the mast, a man can sit well back on the board so that it protects him from painful contact between mast and crutch – there is no such protection with a soft canvas chair.

If no proper bosun's chair is available it is possible to improvise with a fender. Assuming there are eyes at both ends of the fender a line is looped from end to end to form a sling. An eye is seized in the centre and the halyard shackled on. It is essential to use an eye like this to stop the chair slipping sideways and capsizing. Remember to pass the line right under the fender (lengthwise) just in case something goes wrong; you are then at least sitting in a rope sling.

You can actually omit the fender and use a plain rope sling made with a bowline on the bight, but it is most uncomfortable to sit in. Should you be forced to use it I would advise padding yourself with a cushion.

One very important point when preparing a bosun's chair for work at the masthead is to ensure that the halyard is fastened to the chair below chin level. If it is any higher you will have to work with your hands constantly above your head and you may not even be able to see what you are doing. It is essential to fasten the halyard to the chair with either a screw pin shackle or, if a snap shackle is used, to tape over it so there is no chance of the piston snagging and opening.

A line is sometimes led from the bottom of the chair to the deck so that if the person being sent aloft loses contact with the mast he can be hauled back. It can also be used to hold him clear should the need arise, for instance if he wants to work on the outboard end of a spreader.

When the man aloft is going to have to work his way slowly down the mast doing jobs here and there, rather than keep a crewman standing by to lower him occasionally, if an all rope external halyard is used he can bring himself down with a gantline hitch or self-lowering hitch. This is a perfectly secure knot to hang on, but by working the fall through it he can lower himself gently. To stop, all he has to do is tighten the hitch – if his grip slips the hitch will take up

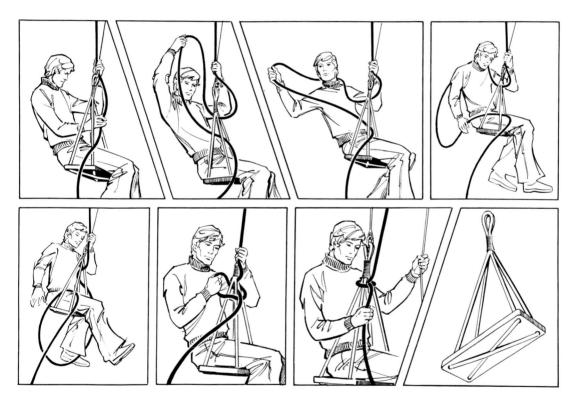

automatically and stop him falling.

To form the gantline hitch hold the working part of the halyard and the fall together in one hand. Reach through the sling of the chair and pull a bight of the fall through towards you. Pass this over your head, drop it down over your body, lift your feet through it and bring it up to the top of the sling, taking up the slack

FIG. 16

A man sitting in a bosun's chair forms a gantline hitch with the fall of the halyard round the apex of the chair's sling. This hitch allows him to move himself down the mast and stop wherever he requires. Note the crossed over parts of the sling under the seat of the chair and the seizing at the apex of the sling.

as you do so. Work the hitch tight at the apex of the sling and there you are. To lower yourself you ease the fall back through the hitch and slip down, inch by inch. To stop you simply stop threading the fall through.

Where no mast winch is available or it is rather small and you do not want to rig up a system of blocks to get the halyard fall back to a cockpit winch, it is quite easy to send a man aloft if he helps you haul. He sits in the chair and grips the fall above his head while you also take a hold, and you haul in unison. This can only really be done in harbour when it doesn't matter that the person in the chair is not holding onto the mast. If it has to be tried at sea it is better for him to haul on the mast or rigging to take some of his weight, but it must still be co-ordinated with the person on the halyard.

Don't cleat the halyard with a man aloft, instead hold it securely round a cleat or with several turns on a winch barrel. He can then be raised or lowered quickly, no-one can cast the halyard off in ignorance of the fact that someone's up the mast, and *he won't be forgotten*. It may sound daft but it has happened that someone has been sent aloft, the halyard made up, the crew gone off to do something else and the poor fellow up the mast left there for hours until someone missed him. If you should need to leave a man aloft unattended, at least give him a whistle with which to summon assistance.

When using a winch to send a man aloft there are two golden rules: don't get a riding turn on the winch and do watch him. For the man at the masthead a riding turn can be a terrifying prospect, after all he can't go up or come down. Unless it can be cleared he has somehow got to transfer to another halyard and come down on that. It needs little imagination to appreciate the horror of the situation if there is any sort of sea running.

With two people on the winch one should wind the handle and the other should tail and watch the person in the chair. The man aloft calls out that he wants to be moved up or down, the watcher repeats the demand and gives directions to the handle man, either to wind in or to check the line out (using the heel of his hand on the turns like any other surging operation). When the person in the chair starts work, it is safer if the handle is taken out of the winch and the person tailing stands well away from the mast. He can still keep a sharp eye on the person aloft but at the same time he should be clear of any dropped tools. To move the chair either up or down return to the mast and work from there.

From a safety point of view a second halyard bent onto the chair will serve to back up the one on which the chair is hoisted. The fall is hitched to the strop of the chair so that the person aloft can adjust it as he is moved up and down.

All tools should have wrist lanyards and if any are carried up in a bucket attached to the chair or in one sent up on a separate halyard, be careful that the bucket does not catch on something, capsize and drop the lot.

In anything of a sea the person going aloft in a chair should wear full oilskins and if possible a lifejacket to protect his ribs from injury if he is swung in hard against the mast. Boots too give protection and some grip.

## Cloggies and Jumars

These are two similar devices developed for use by mountaineers. As applied to boats, they allow a man to hoist himself to the masthead on an all rope halyard, stop and work at any point, then lower himself to the deck again.

The cloggie (it is the simpler, cheaper version) is attached by a short strop to the sling of a bosun's chair and the fall of the halyard passed down through it between a toothed cam (like that on a jamming cleat) and the metal body. The person in the chair hauls on the halyard, holds it and slips the cloggie up to the limit of its strop. He then takes another pull, slides the cloggie up and so on. At any time he can stop and rest simply by letting go. Assuming the halyard does not

part (and we must make some optimistic assumptions about this business) the furthest he can drop is the length of the strop. This must be kept short or the cloggie will come up to the masthead sheave before the sling of the chair and you will not be able to reach the masthead.

Lowering is harder than climbing as the person in the chair has to haul himself up a little to take the strain off the cloggie then release the cam and hold it open to let the halyard slide through.

## Ladders

These are not really as good for going up masts as they sound because they twist round making it very hard to get your feet on the rungs. There is a plastic ladder available called the Mastep which is designed as either a boarding ladder or for going aloft. It gets over the twist problem by being lashed to the mast, but this can only be done of course when no mainsail is set. One very good point is that it has brackets to hold the rungs clear of the mast, and that makes climbing much easier. Like any ladder it must be hoisted to the masthead and then bowsed down really hard to stop it swinging and to reduce twisting.

Rope ladders are easy to make and it is best to use a stiff rope so that they hold their shape. Rungs can be made with the rope, but better is to use bars of wood held in place with marline spike hitches. Don't use clove hitches as they allow the bar to roll when it is stepped on. The bars should be about a foot long and spaced about 15 in.

## Mast steps

On boats over about 30ft (say 9m) there is no doubt that steps attached to the mast are the answer to the problem of going aloft. These metal brackets must not be spaced too widely or climbing becomes difficult, but you are independent of halyards and you can still go aloft even if the top part of the mast has been lost. You have both hands free to hold on while climbing and the boat's rolling is less likely to throw you about than it is when you're in a chair or on a ladder. There is also nothing to rouse out or set up, the steps are ready all the time.

For easy masthead work it is worth fitting two steps at the same height so you can stand comfortably on both feet rather than with one leg straight and the other bent. The ultimate I suppose is to fit a mini pair of spreaders a couple of feet below the masthead so that you can sit down to work.

For safety's sake wear a lifeharness and clip the line either straight onto one rung so that you can only fall the length of the line, or round the mast to help hold you close in.

## Ratlines

These used to be a common sight on boats but are not seen so much these days. Whether fitted as lines or wooden bars across the lower shrouds, they offer an easy climb to the spreaders, but that's as far as you go. The other drawback with wooden ratlines is that they chafe sails badly unless carefully protected. They do of course add a bit to windage too, but they are worth consideration.

## Reeving new halyards

With external halyards this presents little difficulty as the new one is taken up (hitched onto the bosun's chair), passed through the sheeve and brought down to the deck. Internal ones are more difficult as a messenger must usually be sent down inside the mast first and then used to reeve off the new line.

A short length of bicycle chain is very convenient for weighting the messenger as it will bend easily round the sheaves. Secure a thin line to it, feed it in at the top of the mast, lower it down and then hook it out at the foot with a bent wire. This part is rarely as easy to do as it is to describe, but it is possible.

Failing any bicycle chain, thin pieces of lead can be used or a large shackle pin might be heavy enough.

Once the messenger has been successfully passed, the new halyard is fastened to it and sent down. This may be done by stitching the line to the halyard if the latter is braided, or by working the light line into the lay of a three strand halyard as though splicing. The important thing is to try to lead the messenger off the end of the halyard not its side. If it comes off the side the halyard will be very hard to lead out of the lower sheave.

# CHAPTER TEN

# MAN OVERBOARD

There are two jobs when a man goes overboard. One is to find him and the other is to recover him. Everyone worries about the first of these, and rightly so, but it could very well prove to be the second that is the more difficult task.

## Location

If a person is seen to fall overboard someone must immediately be detailed to keep their eyes on him. This must be their sole responsibility during the rescue operation from which no one is allowed to distract them. This must be emphasized. It is extremely easy to lose sight of a head bobbing amongst even the smallest waves and, once lost, it may be a considerable time before the person in the water is spotted again, during which time he will have got colder and weaker making recovery more difficult.

Assuming no one saw the person go overboard a search must be mounted immediately he is missed. Exactly how this will be conducted depends on the boat, her crew and the conditions of wind and sea at the time, but it must be a systematic search following a carefully rehearsed pattern.

If you are on a dead run when someone

FIG. 17
Search patterns to be adopted when a man has gone overboard and been lost to view.

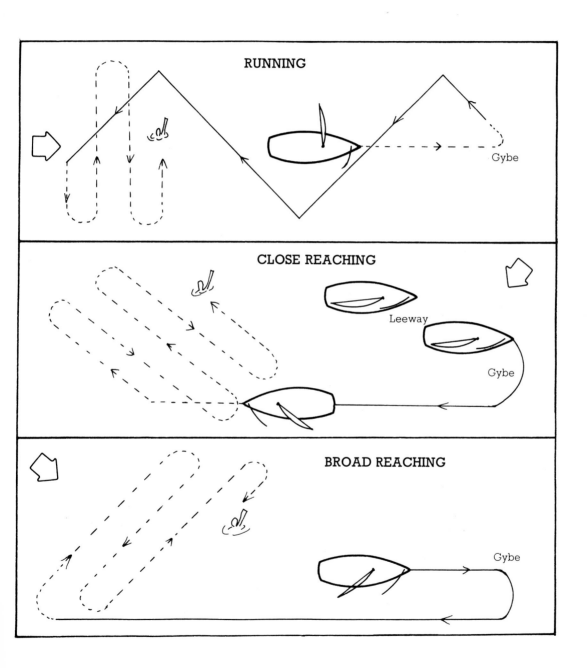

RUNNING

CLOSE REACHING

Leeway

Gybe

BROAD REACHING

Gybe

goes overboard you will have to turn the boat and beat back. Sail each board for an equal length of time and try to work out roughly how far back the man in the water could be. Take the most pessimistic account of when anyone last saw him and work out how far you have run since then. What you are trying to do is ensure that you beat back *past* where he probably is. Once you are sure you have passed him, gybe and sail back down wind in a series of equal-time beam reaches.

Just how long each tack and later each beam reach should be is hard to say. It must depend on the speed of the yacht and the conditions of visibility, you will have to use your own judgement. The idea is to cover an equal area of sea on each side of your original course, hoping as you do so to spot the man in the water. Or indeed to hear him, and this is another important point, try to listen in case he calls or uses a whistle attached to his lifejacket. Don't flash torches around at night as you will destroy night vision, but if someone thinks they hear something it may be worth letting that person alone use a torch while everyone else covers their eyes. I'm not sure.

If you are on a close fetch when someone falls overboard the boat will probably be making some leeway. This can be compounded by gybing so that you *know* you are to leeward of the person in the water. The best plan now is to sail back on a broad reach until you are again as certain as you can be that you have gone past him, then return on a series of beam reaches across the original course line. Each of these reaches should be timed carefully, though it is once again impossible to offer a rule about how long they should be.

This is the main problem with any man overboard situation – there are no hard and fast rules that will always work. You have to make the best of a very bad situation and do a hell of a lot of praying. Even when you do find him your troubles are far from over – so are his.

A broad reach situation can be treated in much the same way as a close fetch, by gybing to put the boat to leeward of the man in the water then sailing back on a close fetch. Once you think you're past him turn onto a series of timed beam reaches working down wind.

In each of these cases as soon as the person is sighted one crewman must be given the job of watching him. It may help the helmsman if the watcher points at the man overboard all the time, otherwise he must be ready to point the direction whenever asked.

There is the possibility of motoring back to search for someone in the water, but I feel that if you are under sail at the time of his going overboard you are better to remain that way at least until he has been located. Following the patterns described is probably easier under sail than power and you can listen for a call which the engine would drown. If you are under power at the time however, you can best turn and motor back along a reciprocal course hoping to sight the person in the water. If you miss him then you must return in a series of timed runs across the course.

The inevitable question must be what happens if you don't find him after all this? Really I don't know, I suppose you can only repeat the search moving the area to allow for his drift in the water, but do try to keep a mental picture going of where you are in relation to where he could be. If there are other vessels about you can hoist an O flag or signal O in morse with a torch to tell them you have a man overboard. You can radio for help if you carry radio equipment, or you can use flares to call for assistance, but you may just have to go on and on searching.

## Recovery

If someone falls over the side while wearing a lifeharness, it is far easier for them to get back on board if the boat is kept moving with them to leeward. While the boat is moving the person in the water is towed along on the surface and it is not too difficult for him to reach up to the rail and haul himself back aboard. As soon as the boat stops the person in the water has to swim to stay afloat and then haul himself (or be hauled) up the full height of the topsides as a dead weight.

The person must not be towed for too long or too fast (about 4 knots seems right) or he will get cold and lose his strength. It should be obvious that, if he is swallowing a lot of water or is struggling unsuccessfully to get on board, you must stop the boat and try another method of recovery.

Assuming that your search is successful and someone does spot the man in the water, it is probably best to give that person the job of keeping the man in sight. Immediate action must then be to slow the boat and decide how to approach him. Ignore recovery for a minute, try to get a buoyancy aid of some sort into his hands – a lifebuoy, lifejacket or floating cushion, something that is easy to see and hold onto. Remember that from his point of view an object floating with about a couple of inches of freeboard is hidden by a wave only 6in high, so you will have to get it close to him.

One way of doing this which seems to work well is to drop over a lifebuoy with a floating line attached and then encircle the person in the water. That way you can draw the buoy to him so that he does not have to swim after it, but once he has it within his reach you must stop the boat or you will drag it away from him.

Now you can set about the recovery. Don't let the person whose duty it is to watch the man relax, he could still be lost. Also, don't slow up, the longer a person is in the water the colder and weaker he gets, making recovery aboard more difficult and physical recovery less certain.

One tremendously encouraging development of the last two or three years has been the widening acceptance of permanently mounted boarding ladders on the transom. Though they are not always very sightly, they help a lot in overcoming the problems of climbing aboard the modern high freeboard yacht, whether in the normal process of getting out of a tender or in the recovery of a person from the water.

Ideally the ladder should extend well below the waterline, either by having rungs fitted to the underwater hull or a fold-down extension of the ladder. This allows a person in the water to step on the bottom rung without having to raise one foot to the level of his chin – not an easy action at the best of times, let alone when you're half drowned.

As an alternative to a ladder, steps fitted to a transom hung rudder are another excellent idea, but these again should extend well below the waterline.

In the absence of a boarding ladder, or if he is incapable of climbing one, the best method I know of recovering someone from the water is to launch a half inflated dinghy and get him into that, then pick him up from there. Even a very weak man can be helped in over the deflated portion by someone getting into the dinghy and pushing the material down under him. The inflated half should support them both, but a sensible precaution would be to tie a line round the man's waist before putting him into the dinghy. Once in the dinghy a short rest period can be allowed and the man then helped aboard.

Before going alongside anyone in the water under power, take as much way off the boat as possible and *stop the engine*. Just putting it in neutral is not enough, it can easily be kicked into gear by accident and you cannot be certain that there is no propeller creep. You don't want to cut off his feet, do you?

The other thing to do as you come alongside is drop the guardrails right down to the deck and warn everyone that this has been done. If you are hove to under sail, bring the man alongside to leeward as the rail will be close to the water and he will have to be lifted a shorter distance.

Permanent steps up the transom or a rigid boarding ladder extending below the waterline are both of immense help in getting anyone out of the water or indeed out of a partially inflated dinghy. If the person has been in the water any length of time he will of course be weak and uncoordinated and it may be very hard for him to climb. For this reason the first action of getting him alongside should be to try to secure a line round his body. It won't be easy work but it will keep him from being swept away from the boat and should help in getting him aboard.

The weight of an exhausted man, especially with a lot of waterlogged clothing, is very great and there's not a lot of room for people to work, so be careful not to fall in yourself. It may be necessary to use a halyard and try to winch him aboard, or at least bring him up nearer to the gunwale and take some of his weight. If he can only be got that far it will be easier to get hold of his clothing and drag him aboard. I think it's that first effort of getting him up so that his waist is on a level with the toerail that is the hardest part. One other way of doing this is to take the mainsail out of its luff track and push the bunt of it into the water. If the person can get onto the sail and lie there, the halyard can be winched up so that he rolls up towards the deck. Keep the mainsheet hardened in and be aware of the fact that it will be hard to get the man onto the sail – it tends to billow in the wind and is hard to sink. It *can* work though, and that's all we can ask of any system.

Once a person has been recovered from the water, treat them for shock. Wrap them up warmly in a sleeping bag and if they want it let them drink hot, sweet tea (or coffee) but *do not give them alcohol*.

This is a rather gloomy subject to close a book on, but it is a horrifying experience for both the person in the water and those left on board. No one knows all the answers about locating and recovering a man overboard, but you should now have some food for thought and discussion. Do work out your own systems and practice them, it is certain to help if the real thing should ever happen, but be warned, it may be a lot harder to get the person out of the water than you ever imagined.

After playing the part of the man in the water during a number of (thankfully successful) practical experiments in search and recovery methods, I sincerely hope that someone will one day find a foolproof solution to all the problems. Until then the advice must be, don't fall overboard – or if you do, wear a lifeharness.

# INDEX